BECOME A BETTER THINKER

BECOME A BETTER THINKER

4TH EDITION

DR JOHN LANGREHR

amba
press

First edition published by Wrightbooks in 1994.
Second edition published in 1995.
Third edition published in 2001.
This edition is published by Amba Press in 2022.

Amba Press
Melbourne, Australia
www.ambapress.com.au

Cover Designer – Tess McCabe

Printed by IngramSpark

ISBN: 9781922607324 (pbk)
ISBN: 9781922607331 (ebk)

A catalogue record for this book is available from the National Library of Australia.

CONTENTS

ACKNOWLEDGEMENTS

Thanks to publisher Alicia Cohen of Melbourne's Amba Press for having the courage to publish a book on student thinking. Educational decision makers and publishers worldwide continue to focus on what to learn and not on how to learn.

Thanks also to Geoff Wright, owner of Wrightbooks, who also believed and encouraged me by publishing the first edition of *Become a Better Thinker* in 1994.

And thanks to my wife Jan – a true believer, critic, and supporter.

ABOUT THE AUTHOR

Dr John Langrehr is a world-renowned author and researcher with a keen interest and special focus on developing and evaluating creative and critical thinking. He has taught in US and Australian universities over the past 30 years.

Dr John Langrehr also speaks at national and international thinking and gifted conferences. The John Langrehr Thinking Program (JLTP – www.jltp.net) is a unique program specially developed by Dr Langrehr for young children.

Dr Langrehr has written over 25 books. Many have been published in America, Canada (French), Australia, Singapore, China, India, Malaysia, Mexico and Saudi Arabia (Arabic). He is delighted to be publishing the 4th edition of his most well-known book, *Become a Better Thinker*.

PREFACE

It was at university where I read about the work of Benjamin Bloom. He suggested that there were six quite different levels of thinking. The first four levels of lower order thinking dominate most classroom thinking. They stimulate and develop correct answer thinking or remembering. The last two levels, called higher order or multiple answer thinking, are now needed more than ever in our rapidly changing world that is flooded each day with new information.

About 20 years ago I went to my first International Conference on Critical Thinking at Sonoma State University in California. I was inspired to lead the charge in Australia. Geoff Wright, owner of Wrightbooks gave me the first start by publishing the first edition of *Become a Better Thinker*.

Now I thank Alicia Cohen, publisher and owner of Amba Press, for her encouragement and support in helping all student to think better for themselves. Even our government has this belief by making creative and critical thinking a priority in the Australian Curriculum.

It is still a fight to get better thinking in our classrooms. Teachers and students need better materials to actually make better student thinking a reality. Initial teacher education courses need to place more emphasis on topics covered in this book. These include metacognition, pattern recognition, brain functioning, question designing, and thinking styles.

I have tried to win the fight by presenting at over 50 conferences, by writing over 50 articles in teacher magazines, and by writing over 25 books on thinking with the help of 12 publishers and 4 translations. Things are changing but teachers need encouragement and practical resources. School leaders need better understanding of what thinking is all about. I hope this book will help all readers to carry on the fight for BETTER THINKING in our schools.

John Langrehr
2022

CHAPTER 1

INTRODUCING THINKING

Pre-reading questions to ponder:

- What is thinking?
- Why don't school programs teach students how to think to their full potential?
- Can we find out how good thinkers think?
- What are some basic thinking processes we use each day?
- How is our brain similar to a computer?

WHAT DOES THINKING INVOLVE?

Thinking involves the mental processing of information that we sense, or that we have already stored in our memories. So, much of our thinking involves remembering or 'pulling out' stored information. We can improve remembering with plenty of practice or rehearsal, and with the use of some of the memory aids discussed in Chapter 10. To a certain extent, computers and smart phones have made this kind of thinking less important these days.

However, much of our thinking is more complex. It involves analytical, creative and critical thinking. These kinds of thinking require us to ask ourselves questions in order to form physical-neural-links between new and old stored information.

Thinking is vital in the 21st century.

SCHOOLS AND THINKING

Most school programs focus on teaching students content and methods to remember knowledge. They aim to develop the Content Intelligence of students for examination purposes. They emphasise the 'What to think about' much more than the 'How to think about it'!

However, a good memory for prescribed facts and methods is no longer a guarantee for a successful life after school. And it is no longer a guarantee for creating a competitive and imaginative future generation for a nation. Therefore, many more school programs need to help all students to ask themselves better questions about the content they are taught. How many questions were you taught for distinguishing a fact from an opinion, a definite conclusion from an indefinite one, a relevant factor from an irrelevant one, or a good generalisation from a poor one?

These are just four of the 20 or so core, or basic, thinking processes that educators and academics have agreed that we use most days to analyse and judge information. How can we understand and critically read a newspaper, a report, a book, or listen to a comment or speech if we don't have a good grasp of the entire range of core thinking processes? A list of these thinking processes is included in this chapter (see pages 5–7). How many can you use with any confidence?

METACOGNITION

At this point you might be asking, 'How can I learn some good questions in order to have a grasp of the core thinking processes?' The answer lies in the process of metacognition. Research of 170 studies over 50 years shows metacognition to be the most powerful factor for improving the thinking and learning ability of students.

Metacognition allows us to 'get inside' the minds of good thinkers in order to find out their feelings and the questions they ask themselves during a task. They share these things by carefully reflecting on them and then saying them out loud.

An example of the use of metacognition for identifying good questions for the process of problem solving is presented in Chapter 2.

THE BRAIN AND COMPUTERS

Our laptop or computers are very good at pattern recognition and probing. But before they can do such things they require a series of questions to be fed into them via programs and instructions. Then, and only then, can our computers rapidly ask themselves questions, created by computer programmers, to correct spelling, problem solve, do statistics, and so on. In other words, typing content or data into computers, without the appropriate processing questions to think about this content, is a waste of time.

And so it is with the super computer that we each own, namely our brain. There is good evidence that the brain is made up of three quite different general intelligences:

- ◆ Tactical Intelligence
- ◆ Emotional Intelligence
- ◆ Content Intelligence.

These three interacting intelligences are stored in different parts of our brains. It has been suggested that our processing questions, that make up our Tactical Intelligence, are mainly stored in the hippocampus of the brain, and some areas of the frontal lobes. Positive, negative and neutral feelings, which make up our Emotional Intelligence, are stored in the amygdala of the brain. They are connected to the Content Intelligence, stored in the cortex, or crinkled grey matter of the brain, by thousands of connections. If these connections are cut we lose our feelings!

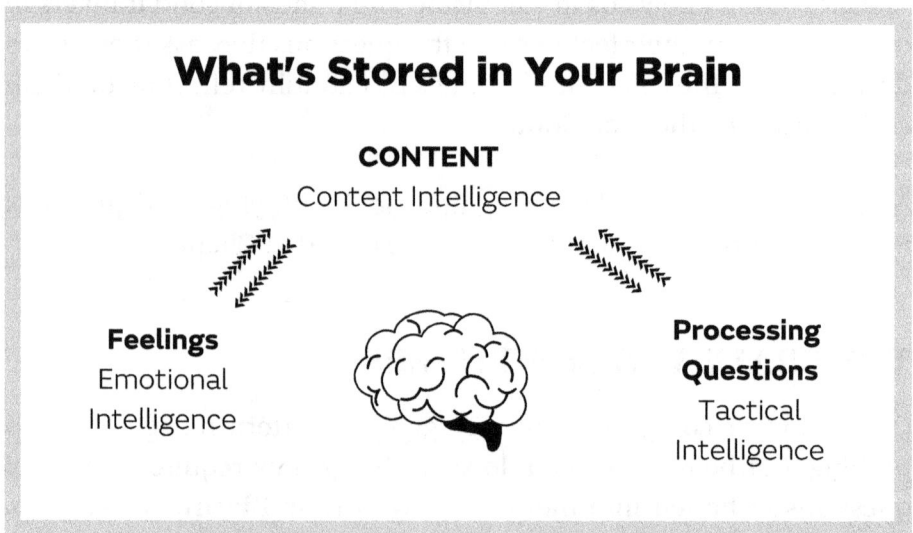

What's Stored in Your Brain

CONTENT
Content Intelligence

Feelings
Emotional
Intelligence

**Processing
Questions**
Tactical
Intelligence

Of course, the human brain is different from a computer in that it has a degree of positive or negative feeling towards any content it is processing. These feelings make up our Emotional Intelligence. This most important intelligence limits our other intelligences and will be discussed further in Chapter 3.

When we have an extreme feeling about an experience, a person, a subject, and so on, we store not only the 'content' but also the positive, negative or neutral feeling we associate with it. We grow a physical link between the content and the feeling.

Another difference between the brain and a computer is the ability of the brain to create and store mental images or pictures of information in order to summarise and clarify it. We all have the ability to create our own unique picture of some common information depending on our interest and experience of the content in the information. Mental images and the graphic organisers they become when they are sketched onto paper are discussed in Chapter 6.

Programs exist to develop all three of our intelligences. Minimal formal time is given to the development of Tactical Intelligence and Emotional Intelligence in the school curriculum and yet they limit the use of our Content Intelligence.

CORE THINKING PROCESSES

Here are some of the core or basic thinking processes that we use each day to question information that we see and hear. When we use any of these thinking processes we ask ourselves a series of questions.

Core Thinking Processes
From Robert Mazarno (1988) *Dimensions of Thinking: A Framework for Curriculum and Instruction.* Association for Supervision and Curriculum Development.

1. Observing properties

2. Observing similarities

3. Observing differences

4. Categorising similar things

5. Identifying non-examples of a category

6. Comparing

7. Sorting things into categories

8. Organising things in order of their size

9. Organising things in order of time

10. Generalising about examples

11. Verbal summarising

12. Visual summarising

13. Analysing relationships

14. Analysing patterns in sequences

15. Visually analysing given data

16. Visually representing properties

17. Distinguishing facts, non-facts and opinions

18. Distinguishing definite from indefinite conclusions

19. Challenging the reliability of claims

20. Distinguishing relevant from irrelevant information

21. Thinking critically about things you read

22. Making decisions

23. Identifying causes and effects

24. Considering other points of view

25. Reverse creative thinking

26. Analysing the creativity of designs.

KEY POINTS

☑ To think better you first have to learn to ask yourself some better questions.

☑ You can ask good thinkers to tell you the kinds of questions they ask themselves when thinking in specific ways. This is called metacognition.

☑ Metacognition is the most powerful way for improving thinking and learning. This is because you can learn what passes through the mind of good spellers, problem solvers, good managers, and people who are good at creative and critical thinking.

☑ We use up to 20 to 30 core thinking processes each day to process information. We can learn useful self-questions for each of these core thinking processes.

CHAPTER 2

THE 4 Ps OF GOOD THINKING

Pre-reading questions to ponder:

- ◆ What do good thinkers have in common?
- ◆ Why is pattern recognition important when thinking?
- ◆ Why do we need to be positive when we think?
- ◆ Why do we need to ask ourselves questions when we think?
- ◆ Why is mental picturing important in thinking?

DIFFERENT WAYS OF THINKING ABOUT A PROBLEM

We all have different thoughts when solving a common problem. This activity, is a problem that illustrates this claim. To approach this problem:

- Read through the problem.
- Note down any thoughts that you have before attempting to solve it.
- Reread the problem.
- Did you have any new thoughts about its wording or information?
- Go ahead and try to solve the problem.

Activity

Tom, Dick, Jan, and Tina are each wearing a different coloured shirt. The colours are red, blue, orange, and yellow. Tom is not wearing red. Dick is not wearing red or blue. Jan is in yellow. What colour shirt does each have on?

Tom   Dick

Jan   Tina

After your attempt, go back and carefully list the specific, short, and unconscious questions that passed through your mind during and after this mental task.

THE FIRST 'P' FOR GOOD THINKING: POSITIVITY

Here are some typical thoughts from the many people who have tried this problem.

Weak Positivity	Strong Positivity
I'm going to hate this. Why do I need to do this? I'm no good at problem solving.	I love these problems. This is going to be fun. I must keep at it until I solve it.

Well, what do this first group of thoughts relate to? If you said attitude, disposition towards the task or motivation, you are on the 'right' track. Yes, they all relate to the degree of positivity a thinker has towards a mental task. The first three thoughts obviously come from poor problem solvers. They show the negativity, or poor positivity, these people have towards problem-solving tasks. This attitude possibly comes from the past failure they have experienced when solving problems.

Positivity, the first important 'P' for good thinking, affects such things as our motivation, persistence, and the focus we have towards a task. Naturally, success in doing a task will improve our positivity. The more successes, the greater our positivity towards a particular type of thinking.

In Chapter 3 you will learn that, apart from success, the best strategy for improving positivity is to learn some positive thoughts to say to yourself before and during a specific task. Sports coaches and psychologists are experts at using this strategy. They feed many positive thoughts into the minds of their athletes before a competition. By saying encouraging thoughts over and over to themselves, athletes improve their focus, and their desire to succeed. Their adrenalin levels are heightened, inducing greater muscle efficiency.

THE SECOND 'P' FOR GOOD THINKING: PATTERNS

Here is a second group of thoughts for the problem solving task. What are they about?

Weak Pattern Seeking	Strong Pattern Seeking
The boys names are first. The colours are not in alphabetical order.	The problem is about 2 variables – people and colour choices.

These thoughts relate to the patterns people see in information. Poor thinkers see very few, if any, patterns in information. If they do sense patterns they usually aren't very helpful in completing the task. The first two patterns here concerning the order of names and the order of colours are not particularly helpful in solving this problem.

The last observation concerning two variables is helpful because it gives a clue as to the shape of a visual diagram or map for the problem. This is needed for summarising the data given and hence solving the problem.

A good problem solver is quick to recognise this problem as a two-variable problem. This then suggests the need for a two-dimensional table on which to summarise the data given.

Effective pattern seeking is the second important 'P' needed for good thinking.

THE THIRD 'P' FOR GOOD THINKING: PROBING

Here is a third group of thoughts that people often think when solving this problem-solving activity.

Weak Probing	Strong Probing
Maybe Tom is wearing blue? Maybe someone isn't wearing a shirt? Is there a trick here? Why are we given Jan's colour?	What do I have to find? Have I done something like this before? What am I given? Are there any limits given here? What do I have to be careful of in these problems? What, if any, formulae do I have to use?

These thoughts relate to the probing, or the silent asking of questions to yourself in order to 'connect' new information to old related information that you have already stored in your memory. The questions are vital processing questions. It is important to ask yourself questions concerning incoming information in order to understand it. This helps to link it with stored information that you already know and, in turn, understand the new information.

Poor thinkers ask themselves very few questions about information they are exposed to. On the other hand, good thinkers are continually probing by asking themselves useful processing questions to connect new and old information.

Such processing questions make up a general problem-solving strategy.

Probing Questions Good Problem Solvers Ask Themselves...

▶ What do I have to find? (goal setting)

▶ What am I given? (data checking)

▶ Are there any limits given here? (identifying restrictions)

▶ Have I done something like this before? (recalling past experiences)

▶ What formulae/principles do I have to use here?

▶ What do I have to be careful of in these problems?

▶ Can I use a diagram to help? (planning)

▶ Can I break the problem up into parts?

▶ Can I use simpler numbers/parts?

▶ What is the first thing to do and why? (sequence planning)

▶ What is the next thing to do and why?

▶ What will happen if I do this?

▶ Does this make sense?

▶ How am I going? (monitoring progress)

▶ How much time should I spend here?

▶ Does this check out? (assessing success)

▶ Is there a rule/method I should remember for next time?

Unfortunately, students are rarely taught a range of useful problem-solving processing questions like those in the previous table. And yet, problem solving is a major classroom activity.

Were you ever taught such a list of processing questions for problem solving?

How about a list for learning the spelling of new words or one for creative thinking and one for critical thinking? Unfortunately, many school programs teach students what to think about but not how to think about it. Research shows that when poor problem solvers or spellers are given lists of processing questions their ability to problem solve or spell increases significantly. For the first time these students have been allowed inside the minds of a good problem solver or speller.

Activity   SILHOUETTE

Give your student(s) a fairly difficult word, such as silhouette, for them to remember its spelling.

Ask them to write down any questions they ask themselves about the word that help them to remember its spelling. After a few minutes call for questions used. Create a class list. Make a large poster of the list and permanently display it at the front of the room. Encourage students to keep their own list.

Ask students to learn the spelling of 10 or 20 new words for homework and to use their spelling thinking 'chip' as they focus on each word. Test them on the words. Note any improvement in the class performance and that of individuals who have previously been poor spellers.

How does your list of useful questions to ask yourself when remembering the spelling of a word compare with the 'Probing Questions' I have suggested at the end of this chapter?

Activity

Choose a short reading from a common text about a topic of interest. Before asking the class to read it tell them to note down during, or after, the reading any questions they ask themselves about any words, sentences, or paragraphs in the reading.

After the reading, call for any questions used. Create a class list of questions used for display on a wall chart. Get students to copy the reading questions.

At a later time, give students a reading comprehension piece. Encourage them to use their list of reading questions during the piece. Note any improvement in class and individual reading comprehension due to the use of self-questions that good readers ask themselves.

THE FOURTH 'P' FOR GOOD THINKING: PICTURES

Let's go back to our original activity concerning the four people and the colour of their shirts. A fourth group of thoughts relate to the pictures people visualise to help them solve a problem. People make comments like these below:

Weak Picturing	Strong Picturing
My mind is blank. I can't picture anything.	Can I use a diagram to help me? I will use a table to summarise the data. I will put names along one axis and colours along the other.

Good thinkers in any subject, occupation, sport, or hobby draw mental pictures in their mind to clarify and summarise information. On the other hand, poor thinkers generally have only a fuzzy picture, if any, of the main terms and ideas in a reading or discussion and of how these things are linked together. Imaging is very important in every kind of thinking, whether it be in sport, problem solving, designing, and so on.

In our original activity used to introduce the four Ps of good thinking, once a person draws a two-dimensional table and places the data on the two axes, the problem solves itself.

More will be said about the four Ps of good thinking in the following chapters. For now, remember that good thinkers have four characteristics in common.

Good thinkers:

- Have good positivity towards a task
- Are quick to see relevant patterns in information
- Ask themselves probing questions
- Use picturing to mentally summarise information.

As previously mentioned, creative and critical thinking will be vital for participating in the rapidly changing evolving world. What kinds of positivity, pattern seeking and probing go through the minds of people who are good at these ways of thinking? The answer to these questions follow in the coming chapters.

Probing Questions Good Spellers Ask Themselves...

▶ How many syllables or small words in this word?

▶ What does the word start and end with?

▶ Are there any parts that are going to be tricky to remember?

► Can I form a mental picture that will help me to remember this word?

► Do any parts sound differently from how they are spelled?

► What does this word mean?

► Does this word look like any other word that I know?

KEY POINTS

☑ Good thinking involves a positive attitude, quick pattern recognition, asking yourself relevant probing questions, and the creation of mental pictures for summarising and clarifying the information.

☑ Positivity can be improved by learning groups of relevant positive thoughts to say over and over to yourself.

☑ Pattern seeking can be improved by learning the patterns that good thinkers quickly recognise in information.

☑ Probing, or the asking of relevant self-questions, can be learned from good thinkers through the process of metacognition.

☑ Picturing, or mental imaging, can be improved by learning basic shapes on which to summarise key information.

CHAPTER 3

POSITIVITY

Pre-reading questions to ponder:

- How does a positive attitude help us to think better?
- How can we learn to improve our self-esteem, confidence, and persistence – three vital elements of our emotional intelligence?
- Are there different kinds of positive attitudes for different kinds of thinking?

Some people like to think of our brain as storing three quite different kinds of intelligence:

Content Intelligence is limited by the content we have stored in our in memory to think with.

Tactical Intelligence is restricted by the number of processing questions that make up our basic thinking processes. In other words, the quantity and quality of the questions we can ask ourselves to connect and make sense of new and old content.

Emotional Intelligence is limited by the number of positive thoughts we have linked to different kinds of content, experiences, and various emotions. We somehow store an emotional loading, positive, neutral, or negative, which we associate with most of the content we have stored in our memories. Be honest, what kind of loading have you associated with physics, poetry, Miss Brown the French teacher, football, your self-esteem, or politicians?

EMOTIONAL INTELLIGENCE

Our Emotional Intelligence limits the use we make of both our Content Intelligence and our Tactical Intelligence. If we don't have the right attitude then we can't use our stored content and skills, or our mental processing questions, to their full potential.

Now, we can learn to improve our Emotional Intelligence just as we can learn to improve our Content and Tactical Intelligence. How do we do this? The answer is to learn some important positive thoughts concerning some basic or core emotional skills that, in turn, are associated with Emotional Intelligence. In Chapter 1 we listed over twenty core-thinking processes associated with our Tactical Intelligence. Now, here are nine emotional skills associated with our Emotional Intelligence.

Some Important Emotional Skills

▶ Internal locus of control

▶ Risk taking

▶ Optimism/confidence

▶ Persistence

▶ Self-esteem

▶ Goal setting

▶ Tolerance of others

▶ Time management.

As already mentioned, sports psychologists and coaches plant positive thoughts into the minds of their athletes. This helps them to focus on the task at hand, to be confident, to persist and to increase their adrenaline flow. And yet, teachers and trainers rarely plant positive thoughts into the minds of their students and workers to improve their focus and persistence.

Overleaf are some positive thoughts to help the development of each of the nine emotional skills mentioned above. These thoughts need to be memorised or written down for individuals to remind themselves when contemplating a difficult task.

Positive Thoughts for Some Basic Emotional Skills	
Internal locus of control	"The harder I try the better my results"
Delaying of gratification	"To get good results I might have to do things I don't like doing."
Risk taking	"The greatest mistake is being afraid of making a mistake."
Optimism-confidence	"Making a mistake is not the end of the world."
Tolerance of others	"Everyone has good points, needs friends, and has feelings."
Persistence	"I don't like doing this but I will give it a go."
Self-esteem	"There are some things that I know I am good at."
Goal setting	"Setting small goals gives me a purpose and something to aim for each day."
Time management	"Honestly, what is the shortest time in which I can finish this task?"

For each of these emotional skills, a more detailed list of positive thoughts can be generated. Here are some examples.

Positive Thoughts for Building Confidence

▶ This doesn't have to be perfect.

▶ I've done it before so I can do it again.

▶ So what if I make a mistake, other people make mistakes.

▶ It won't be the end of the world if I can't work this out.

▶ It might take some time but l know I can do it.

Confidence involves thoughts and feelings about being successful. Confident learners trust in their own ability to be successful. On the other hand, students low in confidence give up easily, blame themselves for failure, and predict failure. They are afraid of making mistakes, and rarely take credit for their successes.

Persistence is another important element of our emotional intelligence. Good thinkers persist with a task even if they don't have immediate success. In order for poor thinkers to persist they may need to learn some positive thoughts like those in the persistence builder below.

A Persistence Builder...

▶ I don't like this but I will do it anyway.

▶ It's hard but not impossible.

▶ l haven't learned this yet but I will.

▶ This task may be unpleasant but it will pay off in the long term.

Self-esteem is a third important element of our emotional intelligence that can limit our thinking and learning. It is vital in helping us to focus on a task with confidence and persistence.

Poor self-esteem comes from the continual downgrading of oneself after failed tasks. Failures become too much of a focus and erase any past successes. If you have low self-esteem you might like to learn some of the positive thoughts listed on the self-esteem builder below.

A Self-Esteem Builder...

▶ I am worthwhile because I am me.

▶ I can't please everyone all of the time.

▶ One good thing I have done is...

▶ Things will be better tomorrow.

▶ Everyone makes mistakes. Mistakes are part of learning.

▶ I am not an 'E' person just because l got an 'E' on my test.

All learners should feel confident about improving their ability to think better. If they can't learn some of the positive thoughts previously listed then they should be able to say...

> *"I own a super computer, I am intelligent in at least one way. I can learn to be more intelligent, regardless of my age, if I really want to."*

What are the characteristics of adults with a good overall positivity or high Emotional Intelligence?

- ◆ They tend to know and manage their own emotions
- ◆ They are internally motivated
- ◆ They can recognise various emotions in others
- ◆ They can effectively manage relationhsips with others.

Some researchers talk about us having an EQ (an emotional quotient) as well as an IQ (an intelligence quotient). They have studied many people with a high EQ and have noted various common characteristics.

Characteristics of Adults With High Emotional Intelligence

▶ Socially poised, outgoing, cheerful

▶ Comfortable with themselves and others

▶ Committed to people and causes

▶ Adaptable with respect to stress

▶ Caring in their relationships

▶ Not prone to fearfulness

▶ Ethical in their outlook

▶ Rarely anxious or guilty.

What we have looked at so far are some general positive thoughts learners can say to themselves in order to increase their positivity towards a learning task. The greater the positivity, the greater the attention, motivation, persistence, and confidence a learner has towards pattern seeking, probing, and picturing – the four characteristics of good thinking.

You may think of other kinds of attitude, or positivity, needed for other kinds of thinking. For example, is there another kind of positive attitude needed for selling things, for managing situations, and so on?

Overleaf is a great activity to try with your students.

Activity

1. Ask your students what they think the meaning of 'confidence' is.

2. Ask them to write down the name of a class member who they think is very confident.

3. Ask them to write down some things about that person that tells you he or she is confident.

4. Ask the confident people nominated to tell the class any positive thoughts they have as they try a difficult task. Record a list of their positive thoughts and display it on the board. Encourage students lacking in confidence to say these thoughts over and over to themselves when they lack confidence during a task.

5. Repeat steps 1 to 4 for people with high self-esteem and high persistence.

6. Ask students to talk about any positive thoughts they have been taught by coaches. Have they helped? How?

KEY POINTS

☑ Positivity increases our attention to a learning task, and it helps us to be more confident and persistent with the task.

☑ Our positivity depends on various emotional elements such as self-esteem, confidence, and persistence.

☑ Different kinds of thinking such as creative thinking and critical thinking require different kinds of positive thoughts.

☑ Our Emotional Intelligence limits the use we make of our Content Intelligence and our Tactical Intelligence.

CHAPTER 4

PATTERNS

Pre-reading questions to ponder:

- ◆ Why do different people sense different patterns in the same information?
- ◆ Why do our brains remember patterns?
- ◆ Where are the patterns in words, numbers, pictures, movements, and behaviours?

Good thinkers are quick to sense relevant patterns in information they attend to. On the other hand, poor thinkers sense very few patterns, if any, even when looking at the same information that good thinkers are attending to.

In the previous chapter you saw how a positive disposition was essential in helping you to focus on, or attend to, information. In this chapter you will see how important it is to sense relevant patterns in information before you can ask yourself questions about them. Poor pattern recognition, along with poor positivity, leads to poor thinking and incomplete learning.

DIFFERENT PATTERNS FOR DIFFERENT THINKERS

It is important, at this point, to note that we all have at least seven or eight different kinds of intelligence as suggeted by Harvard psychologist, Howard Gardner. Gardner first outlined his theory in his 1983 book *Frames of Mind: The Theory of Multiple Intelligences*, where he suggested that all people have different kinds of "intelligences".

Gardner suggested that we each have varying degrees of verbal-linguistic, mathematical-logical, musical-rhythmical, body-movement, intrapersonal, interpersonal and visual-spatial intelligence. He later added an eighth, naturalist intelligence and says there may be a few more.

Activity

Rate yourself on a 1 (low) to 5 (high) scale for each of the 8 intelligences:

____ Visual-spatial intelligence

____ Mathematical-logical intelligence

____ Body-movement intelligence

____ Interpersonal intelligence

____ Intrapersonal intelligence

____ Music-rhythmical intelligence

____ Verbal-linguistic intelligence

____ Naturalist intelligence

Can you explain the reasons behind your ratings of your best and weakest intelligences?

Are you strong in all of these intelligences? If not, name one that you are strong in and one that you are weak in. Athletes certainly have a strong physical-movement intelligence but they may have a poor visual or musical intelligence. We are rarely highly intelligent in all of these different ways of looking at intelligence. It all depends on our interests, our past experiences, our opportunities, our families, and so on.

The point here is that people who are very intelligent in a particular way are very quick to sense patterns in information that relates to their strong intelligence. For example, those who love mathematics are quick to sense patterns in numbers and sequences.

Those who are interpersonally intelligent, or who are good at interacting and communicating with other people, are quick to sense patterns in the body language, the likes, and the moods of people they are communicating with.

Here are some examples of types of people who are strong in a particular intelligence. These patterns help them to make judgements about the source of information.

Intelligence	Patterns in	Indicate
Visual	Line, balance	Complexity, appeal
Mathematical	Wording, data, trends, shapes	Problem type, method to use
Physical	Body movements, context	Complexity, mastery
Interpersonal	Body language, emotions, habits	Feelings, interest
Intrapersonal	Personal behaviour	Self-reflection, personal understanding
Rhythmic	Tones, beats, moods	Harmony
Verbal	Words, poems, sentences	Emotion, bias, fact, meaning
Natural	Nature, collecting, identifying.	Patterns, relations with nature

PATTERNS SENSED BY VISUAL-SPATIAL INTELLIGENT PEOPLE

When most people think of patterns they think of visual patterns. These may involve similarities and differences in the shapes, colours, balance, line, and textures of things made by nature or human beings. People with strong visual-spatial intelligence are particularly sensitive to visual patterns.

David Perkins from Harvard University suggested the strategy of 'knowledge as design'. This can be used to help people with low visual-spatial intelligence become more sensitive to human-made and natural designs about them. As he points out, everything has a design or form that fits a particular function.

The strategy here is to simply ask yourself why a particular thing has the shape, colour, size, or material that it has, rather than other possibilities? Of course, you can probe the existence of many other properties of designs apart from the four listed in the activity box below.

People who are visually intelligent often ask themselves questions about patterns in the structure of the designs of nature and of human beings.

Activity

See if you can answer some of these questions.

Why do trees need so many leaves?

Why do pencils generally have 6 sides?

Why do dogs have 4 legs rather than 2 or 6 legs?

Why are stop lights red?

The overall effect of the strategy is to help people observe designs, and patterns in these designs, much more carefully.

I guarantee you will start observing your world in a completely different way. In the process, you will begin to ask the same kinds of questions that the original inventor of human-made designs asked him or herself. You will start to be a visualiser with a strong visual-spatial intelligence.

Whenever you are doing activities that aim to strengthen visual-spatial intelligence, ask someone who is good at doing such tasks to reflect on and talk aloud the patterns they sensed in the activities. You need to get inside the minds of good visualisers if you want to start thinking like them!

PATTERNS SENSED BY MATHEMATICAL-LOGICAL INTELLIGENT PEOPLE

Good problem-solvers have a strong mathematical-logical intelligence. One of the main reasons for this is their excellent ability to recognise patterns in given data. They are quick to see trends in series and tables of numbers as well as various shapes and symbols. They are quick to sense patterns in the wording of a problem. Key words enable them to categorise the type of problem, to predict potential difficulties with this type and to select the best method or formulae for solving it. Math-logical people are able to link difficult tasks with similar problems they have stored in their memories.

As an example, go back to the problem you tried in Chapter 2 concerning the four people and the colour of their shirts. Don't be satisfied listening to the correct answer to a problem. Get a strong math-logical thinker to talk aloud the patterns he or she saw in the wording of the problem and in the given data, as well as the kinds of patterns he or she visualised to summarise or represent the problem.

PATTERNS SENSED BY BODY-MOVEMENT INTELLIGENT PEOPLE

People with a strong body-kinesthetic intelligence are aware of patterns in the movement of their own body and in those of others. Patterns may be found in the body movements of people who excel in a particular sport or hobby. Body-intelligent people notice such things as the balance, the tempo, the positions and the coordination of good sports people, accomplished dancers, and so on. They also notice patterns in the surrounding environment in which movements are taking place.

For example, the good sailor is quick to sense patterns in the wind. The competent golfer notices patterns in the texture of grass on the greens or of sand in the traps. And the good coach is quick to note patterns in the movements of the opposition-where the attacks are coming from, and where the errors are being made.

As with all of the intelligences, if you want to improve aspects of your body-kinesthetic intelligence get someone who is strong in the intelligence to talk aloud the patterns he or she focuses on during a physical task or movement.

PATTERNS SENSED BY INTERPERSONALLY INTELLIGENT PEOPLE

People who are strong in interpersonal intelligence are good at noticing patterns that influence the communication between other people and themselves. For example, teachers, marketing people, managers, sociologists and anthropologists are all strong in this intelligence.

These people are good at sensing patterns in the non-verbal signals or body language of others that tell that they are bored, confused, tired, interested, lazy, and so on. They are also quick to sense patterns in such things as the likes, habits, preferences and movements of others. With this information they can change their style of communication or presentation in order to relate better with others. They notice the kinds of things that turn people on.

Interpersonally intelligent people notice patterns in the way people use power and in the social and cultural values displayed by groups of people. In short, they notice "people differences" via their patterns of behaviour.

PATTERNS SENSED BY INTRAPERSONALLY INTELLIGENT PEOPLE

Some people are good at reflecting on characteristic patterns in their own behaviour. For example, they are sensitive to their own needs, likes, dislikes, feelings and moods. They can link these patterns to experiences in their lives. Such people are said to have a strong intrapersonal intelligence.

PATTERNS SENSED BY RHYTHMICALLY INTELLIGENT PEOPLE

People who work in the media, theatre, advertising and music industries are strong in rhythmic intelligence. They are all good at using patterns in such things as tones, beats, rhythm and vibrations to express moods and feelings. And they are also good at combining patterns in sounds to patterns in visual images.

For those of us who have a limited rhythmic-musical intelligence one of our biggest problems is to learn the symbols, codes, and characteristics of musical sounds before we can start experimenting with them.

PATTERNS SENSED BY VERBALLY INTELLIGENT PEOPLE

People who are strong in this intelligence are fascinated by the sound, shape, combination and meaning of words. This fascination causes them to strongly focus on patterns in letters, words, pieces of writing, poems, speeches, plays and so on. They are sensitive to word patterns that indicate to them particular bias, emotions, humour and other feelings in spoken or written language.

Like all human creations, letters, words, sentences and so on have a form that fits a function. This aspect gives language a 'shape'. People who have a problem with spelling, reading and writing usually have a problem sensing the relevant patterns in words and sentences. They need people with a strong verbal-linguistic intelligence to reflect on, and say aloud, such patterns.

A useful way of remembering word patterns is to link them with visual patterns, especially funny ones.

PATTERNS SENSED BY NATURALIST INTELLIGENT PEOPLE

People who are strong in this intelligence seem to be in love with the natural world. They like to spend time there, they thrive there, they are skilled and confident and comfortable there, and they learn best there – in short, they are nature smart. They show a sense for detail, noticing and delighting in the smallest of nature's gifts and able to readily follow cyclic patterns in nature such as tides, seasons, moon phases, and climate.

PATTERNS THAT CAN BE SENSED AT WORK

In the world of work and business there are patterns to look for in everything from sales figures to the characteristics of customers. You can see patterns in the way certain customers move around the store, in their times of doing business and in their reliability of paying accounts.

Of course, there are also plenty of patterns in the products business people sell. Some products will show patterns of breaking down easily, of being seasonal, of being in high demand, of selling better if positioned in the store differently, and so on. If you are having difficulties with any mental or physical task at work, don't be scared to ask someone who has success with them to reflect on and share the patterns they sense in these tasks.

As you can see, there are all kinds of patterns around us each day. If you are very positive towards a task and you are still having difficulties with it, I suggest you might not be sensing some important patterns in the information involved in the task.

SOME USES OF PATTERNS

Here are a few of the useful things about patterns and their recognition. Pattern recognition allows us to:

- Recognise examples of something
- Recognise similarities and differences between things
- Predict potential properties of something
- Extend those patterns we already have in memory
- Identify errors in words and calculations
- Identify trends in data and events.

WHY DOES THE BRAIN REMEMBER PATTERNS?

The brain is a wonderful recogniser, comparer, and storer of patterns that it senses each day. Through the identification of patterns in examples of something, we build up a mental picture of this thing, which we call a concept or generalisation. Once our brain remembers a pattern it is very difficult for it to let it go. This difficulty in pattern breaking is the reason why some people find it difficult to think creatively.

Concepts or mental images we have of, say, a car, a tree or a poem, contain all of the features common to examples of these things that we have experienced. In this sense, mental generalisations are very helpful because the brain doesn't have to remember all of the properties for every example that we see or hear.

MAPPING PATTERNS

In order to clarify and summarise similar patterns within examples of something, it is sometimes useful to map them on a summary table. This visual representation of them allows you to quickly see common features. For example, what pattern of common features do you see in high fibre food from the examples of food next?

From these examples you probably formed the generalisation or concept that high fibre foods are low in sugar and low in fat.

Food	Processed	Low Fat	Low Sugar	High Fibre
Cheese	Yes	No	Yes	No
Lettuce	No	Yes	Yes	Yes
Apple	No	Yes	Yes	Yes
Cake	No	No	No	No
Baked Beans	Yes	Yes	Yes	Yes

Such a pattern of common features is easily seen by mapping them in this way.

COMPARING PATTERNS AMONGST FRIENDS

Try some of these activities with your friends and students. Afterwards, share the patterns that you would each look for in these situations. Do they reflect different strengths in particular intelligences? What are these intelligences?

Activity

1. Ask your students to choose one or more of the following and then list any patterns they look for when doing the task.

   Judge whether:

   a. The design of a logo or poster is good or not.

   b. A person is interested in what you are saying or not.

   c. There is a good chance of finding fish, crabs, or deer in a location.

   d. A film is good or not.

2. Show the class a photograph, a film, or read them a poem. Ask individuals to tell the class any patterns they sense in these creations that helps them to make judgements about them.

KEY POINTS

☑ The brain is a wonderful recogniser and storer of patterns. There are patterns in words, numbers, pictures, behaviours, movements, music, and so on.

☑ Patterns help us to recognise things, compare them, identify trends, predict properties and select the best method of doing things.

☑ People who are strong in a particular intelligence are quicker at sensing patterns in information related to that intelligence.

☑ If you can't sense useful patterns in information, ask a good thinker to talk aloud the patterns they sense in it.

CHAPTER 5

PROBING

Pre-reading questions to ponder:

- What happens if you don't ask yourself questions when you read or listen to information?
- What are some ways that help us to ask better questions about a certain topic?
- What kinds of questions do good thinkers ask themselves when they read?

QUESTION STARTERS

Good thinkers are good at asking themselves questions about information they attend to.

Good thinkers are good at PROBING information with thinking questions.

5WH is a good memory aid to remind you of some good starts to questions.

Four of the Ws are **WHAT? WHERE?**, **WHEN?**, and **WHO?**

These 4 question starters are used to test your ability to REMEMBER. They test correct answer thinking. They are used in the kinds of questions teachers and students ask in the classroom. And they are used in IQ tests and in national and international science tests of student memories.

If you want to do more than stimulate and test memory you need the question starters W and H or **WHY?** And **HOW?**

These question starters test the ability to THINK for yourself. They test multiple answer thinking because there are more than one possible answer for WHY? and HOW? questions. They are often used to stimulate and test creative and critical thinking. In summary the 5WH starters are...

    WHEN?
    WHO?
    WHERE?
    WHEN?
    WHY?
    HOW?

Here are some sample questions about pyramids that show the difference between questions that simply test memory and questions that test thinking.

What are pyramids?

Where do you find pyramids?

When were the pyramids built?

Who built the pyramids? and

Why were the pyramids built in the desert?

How were the pyramids built so far from stone quarries?

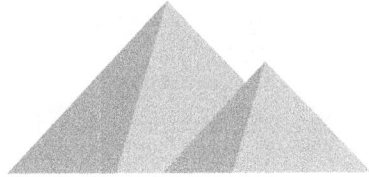

TWO WORD QUESTION STARTERS

The 5WH question starters can be followed by a second word. These include:

IS (present)
DID (past)
CAN (possibly)
WOULD (probably)
WILL (prediction)
MIGHT (imagination)

Some examples of 2 word question starters are

Who is...
Where might...
When will...
What would...

Activity

1. Choose any topic that interests you or your class.

2. Design as many questions about the topic as you can using different TWO WORD QUESTION STARTERS. Share your questions with the class when asked .

3. Who has designed the most questions?
   Who has designed a question that no one else has designed?
   Who has designed a question that no one in the class can answer?

4. Choose another topic and see If you can design 6 questions ... 1 for each of the words on the IS, DID list.

5. You might write the 12 words on the 2 lists here on 12 small cards . Turn the cards over and mix them up. Now choose 1 card from each pile. Try to find an answer for your question.

6. You might have a competition with a friend by choosing 2 cards for your friend to see if they can answer your question. Take it in turns.

PROBING CREATIVE DESIGNS

Most things about us have a special design that fits a particular purpose.

For example , some things have a particular **colour**, a particular **shape**, a particular **material**, a particular **size**, and particular **parts**.

Most people observe the designs or features of things but they rarely ask themselves "Why does this thing have this colour, shape etc"

The questions in this activity are example of the kinds of questions you can ask yourself about any design you observe.

My suggested answers to the questions are in the Appendix A. You may have other answers.

Whatever your answers the questions will make you think. They will make you do some curious thinking.

List 3 possible or acceptable reasons that explain each of the following observations.

1. Most coins are round.

2. Most animals have 4 legs and not 2 like humans.

3. Bees have wings.

4. Fish have scales.

5. Pencils are made of wood?

6. Jars are made of glass?

7. Australian footballs are oval in shape and not round.

8. Flowers are coloured.

9 Elephants have large ears? Hippo's have small ears!

10. Chairs have 4 legs and not 6.

11. Insects are usually very small.

12. Giraffes have very long necks.

13. Newspapers have very large pages compared to the pages of a book.

THE QUESTION MATRIX

The Question Matrix aims to help students design up to 36 questions for a topic they are interested in.

	EVENT	SITUATION	CHOICE	PERSON	REASON	MEANS
PRESENT	1. What Is?	2. Where/ When Is?	3. Which Is?	4. Who Is?	5. Why Is?	6. How Is?
PAST	7. What Did?	8. Where/ When Did?	9. Which Did?	10. Who Did?	11. Why Did?	12. How Did?
POSSIBILITY	13. What Can?	14. Where/ When Can?	15. Which Can?	16. Who Can?	!7. Why Can?	18. How Can?
PROBABILITY	19. What Would?	20. Where/ When Would?	21. Which Would?	22. Who Would?	23. Why Would?	24. How Would?
PREDICTION	25. What Will?	26. Where/ When Will?	27. Which Will?	28. Who Will?	29. Why Will?	30. How Will?
IMAGINATION	31. What Might?	32. Where/ When Might?	33. Which Might?	34. Who Might?	35. Why Might?	36. How Might?

The 6 words... **WHAT, WHERE, WHICH, WHO, WHY, HOW** are placed along the top horizontal axis. They represent the starts to questions.

The 6 words... **IS, DID, CAN, WOULD, WILL, MIGHT** are placed down the vertical axis of the matrix. They represent time or possibility of existence.

Now 36 question starters consisting of the first two words of a question can be formed. For example, WHAT MIGHT? WHERE DID? WHO IS? HOW WOULD?

Any questions formed by the starters in the top horizontal rows are correct answer questions that test remembering and recall. For example, WHAT IS an octogon?

Any questions formed by the starters towards the bottom rows are multiple answer questions that test thinking – particularly creative and critical thinking. For example, WHAT WOULD happen if there were no more bees in the world?

Activity

1. Provide students with access to the Question Matrix.

2. Ask students to use the matrix to design 6 questions on a topic such as dinosaurs. Normally this would be a difficult task for many students without the help of the matrix. After a given time ask students to share a question each with the class. You will be surprised at the range of different questions created.

3. Who has the most interesting question?
   Who has a question that the class can't answer?
   Who has the funniest question?
   Which table of students designed the most questions?

4. Ask students to design 6 questions on a given topic for homework. Get them to try to find answers for their questions. Ask students to share their best questions with the class next day.

PICTURING QUESTIONS TO ASK YOURSELF

When asked to make up a question or two on a nominated topic most people get a little tongue-tied. It is hard to picture a question in your mind. Hence, it is not a bad idea to get in the habit of using some visual devices to help you think up some questions on a topic. Here is an example of such a device.

The Question Map

On the next page is a map for the topic of iron.

The process for sketching the map goes like this:

1. The topic to ask questions about is written in a central box.

2. Key terms related to the topic are written in boxes surrounding the central box. These terms may be brainstormed by a group of people from their existing knowledge of the topic. They could also come from a reading or presentation about a topic.

3. Connectors of between two and five words are written in along each arrow that connects each term to the central topic. These should form a meaningful sentence starting with the topic and ending with a term in an outer box.

4. A question starting with 'Why?' or 'How?' is then asked about each statement made on the map.

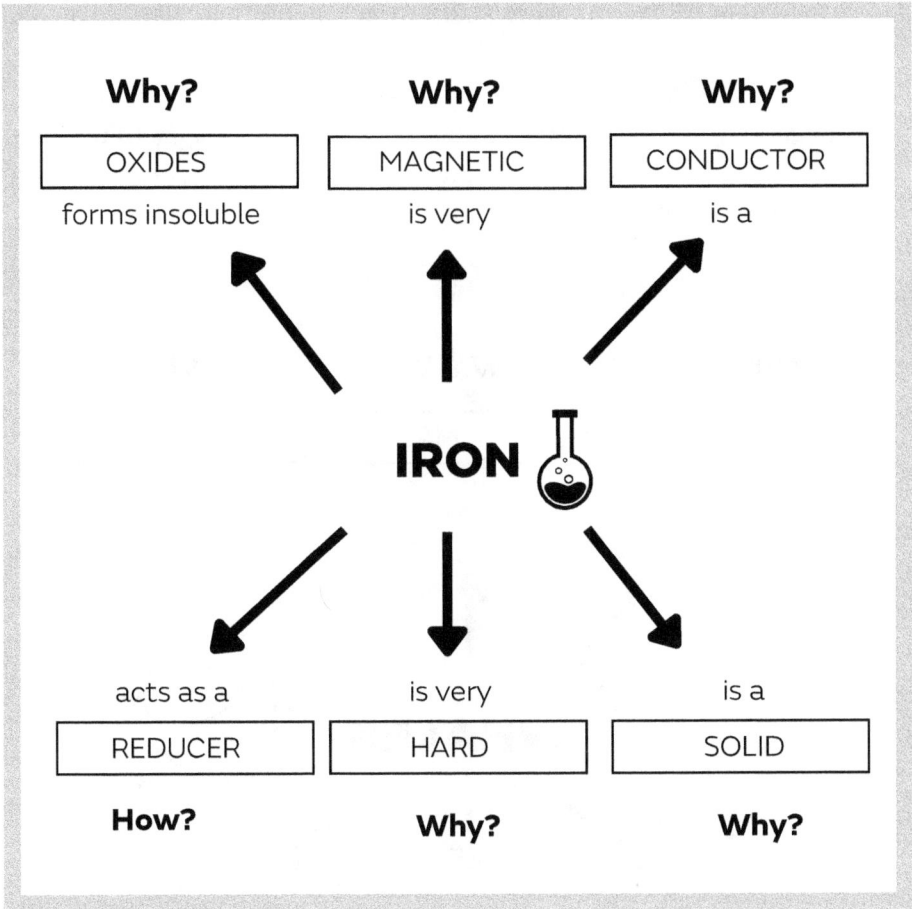

To see how the question map helps to generate some questions, consider another topic such as whales.

1. Write down six or so interesting words that are connected with this topic, e.g. migrate, mammal, baleen, blubber, mouth, communicate.

2. Now write down each of these terms in boxes, surrounding the central topic.

3. Next, write in no more than five words along each arrow to make six meaningful sentences.

4. Finally, ask 'Why?' or 'How?' after each sentence, whichever fits best.

5. Can each of the questions be answered? If not, look them up in an encyclopedia. Notice that we are making new connections for the concept of whales.

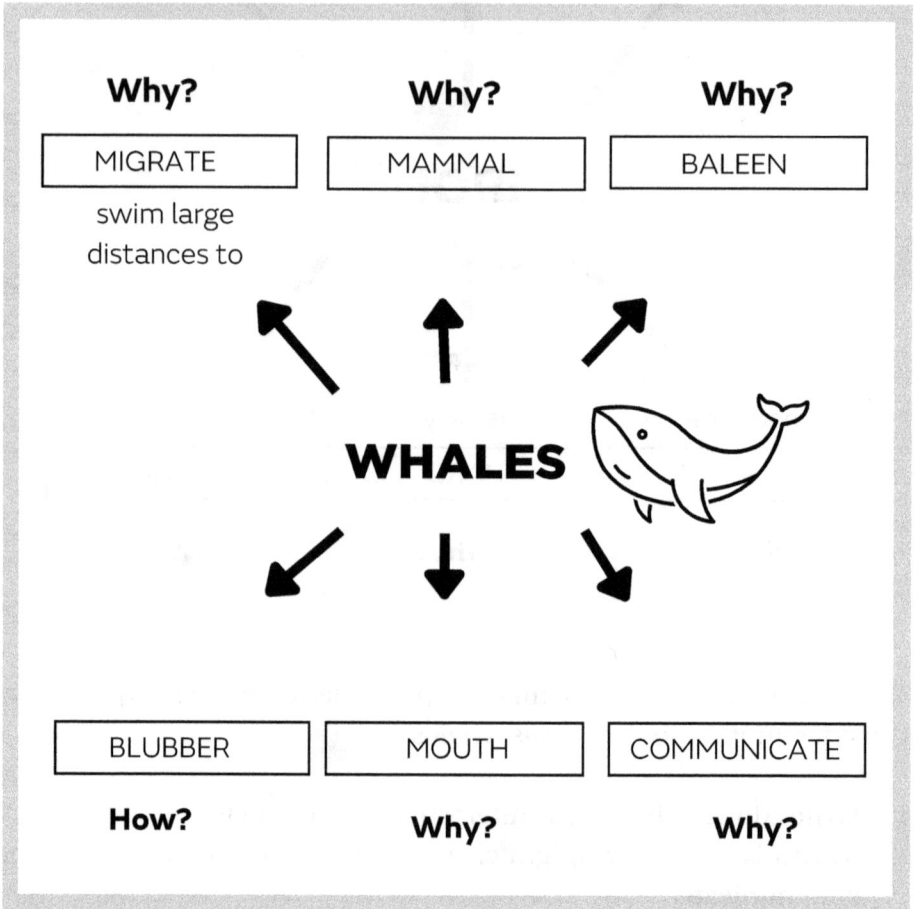

Why?	Why?	Why?
MIGRATE	MAMMAL	BALEEN

swim large
distances to

WHALES

BLUBBER	MOUTH	COMMUNICATE
How?	**Why?**	**Why?**

Here are a few of the useful things about patterns and their recognition. Pattern recognition allows us to:

♦ Why do whales contain so much blubber?
♦ Why do whales have such large mouths?
♦ How do whales communicate with each other?
♦ Why are whales examples of mammals?

MISCONCEPTIONS

Consider the question, 'Why do whales eat baleen?'

This is a misconnection or a misconception. 'Why do whales have baleen?' is better, because baleen is not something to eat.

Misconceptions can play a big part in learning problems. They need to be identified and cleared up before learning some content on a topic. The question map is an excellent device for getting inside the minds of people who have some misconceptions. Faulty connections then become obvious.

EDWARD DE BONO'S SIX HATS

Edward De Bono is one of many people who have tried to develop a system that limits the focus of questions you might ask yourself when thinking about an issue, problem, theme, and so on. His six hat system focuses on questions that relate to six different aspects of a topic or problem.

Black hat	Cautioning questions	Consider negative things or things to check out before making a decision.
White hat	Factual questions	Consider the facts, statistics and data of an issue or problem.
Red hat	Feeling/ emotional questions	Relate to the likes, dislikes, emotions, and feelings of people about an issue.
Yellow hat	Positive questions	Relate to the benefits or positive points of an issue.

Green hat	Creative questions	Relate to alternative and divergent ways of solving a problem or thinking about an issue.
Blue hat	Overview questions	Relate to summarising what has happened or been decided so far.

A manager or group leader can easily ask a group to focus on asking questions that are of a particular colour. For example, green hat questions relate to creative ways of tackling a problem. In this way the whole group will be thinking of alternative or divergent solutions to a problem. The strategy is simple and can be used by anyone to ask themselves quite different questions about an issue or problem.

QUESTIONS WHILE READING

We all have to read from time to time. Sometimes it is a novel, where we just want to enjoy the story rather than continually self-questioning after reading each sentence. However, sometimes we read in order to understand the information presented. This type of reading demands that we question our comprehension of terms, phrases, sentences and paragraphs. During the reading of this chapter a good reader might ask him or herself questions such as:

- ◆ What is this chapter about?
- ◆ What is the meaning of a self-question?
- ◆ What is an example of a self-question?
- ◆ Do I understand this sentence?
- ◆ How can I use metacognition in my work?
- ◆ Could I teach this to someone else?

Chapter 8, on critical thinking, gave you some different types of questions that good critical readers ask themselves when trying to make judgements about something they are reading.

MATHEMATICAL QUESTIONS

Mathematics is one of those subjects where the content or problems gently 'massage' us. This means that many students mechanically do problem after problem with little questioning as to whether they understand the process and formulae used or not. The scenario generally involves the teacher or textbook writer providing some data and also a question for the student to answer.

What happens if the student is given some data and then has to design his or her own question to then find the answer to? For example, here is some data.

> Jack earns $500 a month.
> His expenses are $300 a month.

If the teacher asks the question, 'What fraction of his earnings does Jack spend each month?' the student goes through some mechanical process that he or she has seen the teacher present on the board with many examples. But does the student really understand what is going on? Maybe.

What if the teacher says to the students, 'You design 3 or 4 questions using this data. For each question, state whether you have to use plus (+), minus (-), multiplication (x) or division (÷) operations.' Now the student has to really ask him or herself some questions about the processes of subtraction, division, fractions, percentages and also the sequence in which they are used. The student has to show understanding because he or she is creating the questions rather than simply answering them.

PARTY TIME QUESTIONS

There is a fun way of improving questioning. It aims to help people ask more relevant questions.

Activity

Get someone who will be the questioner to go outside the room. The rest of the group has to decide on the name of someone, some place, some animal, or something in general.

Recall the person and give them a clue as to the category that the name belongs to. For example, a film star, an Australian animal, a country etc.

The questioner has no more than 10 questions to find the answer. They can only ask questions which have a yes or no answer.

This activity teaches us to learn not to waste questions but rather, to think carefully about them, particularly their relevance.

KEY POINTS

☑ Asking yourself questions as you attend to new information helps you to understand it and to connect it to information you have in your memory.

☑ Visual devices such as question maps and question generators help us to visualise and connect information in order to see questions we can ask about a certain topic.

☑ Asking students to design their own questions for some given content helps them to better understand the content and the processes involved.

CHAPTER 6

PICTURING

Pre-reading questions to ponder:

- ◆ What kinds of pictures do good thinkers draw in their minds?
- ◆ Do mental maps have particular shapes?
- ◆ Are mental maps and graphic organisers the same thing?
- ◆ What are the advantages of drawing mental maps on paper?
- ◆ When you read something, how do you know which graphic organiser to choose for summarising the information?

VISUAL MAPS FOR GOOD THINKERS

Good thinkers are good at visualising a problem, a reading, a product, some questions, a physical action, a meeting, and so on. Less productive thinkers either have no picture, or at best a fuzzy one, of information they attend to. We can all learn to become better visualisers.

In this chapter, we will look at some well-known visual map styles that intelligent people use to clarify and summarise the key terms and connections in a reading or presentation. These are actually maps that you can sketch on paper before transferring them to your memory.

EVEN INFORMATION HAS A SHAPE

Groups of key terms or concepts in any piece of writing or speech are usually connected to each other in some geometric pattern or shape.

Verbal information, like other human inventions, has a shape about it.

Therefore, it makes sense to summarise or map terms, together with the way they are connected to each other, on a diagram of a particular shape.

After reading some information, or listening to it being read out loud, good thinkers have a clear picture in their minds of the key terms and ideas discussed and the way they are connected to each other. If they are asked to draw a map or diagram that shows these things, the clarity of their thinking will become apparent.

The quality of the mental maps we store in our minds is limited by the quality of the visual maps we are capable of drawing on paper. There is a skill in visually summarising information on what some people call concept maps or graphic organisers.

There is ample research evidence to show that people who are trained to select and draw visual summarising maps improve their ability to recall and understand information. Such maps apparently increase the likelihood of them having clear and well connected mental maps on a topic.

Here are some standard shapes or graphic organisers for summarising key words and their connections.

CYCLIC MAPS

These maps are used when the key terms in a reading are stages in a cyclic process.

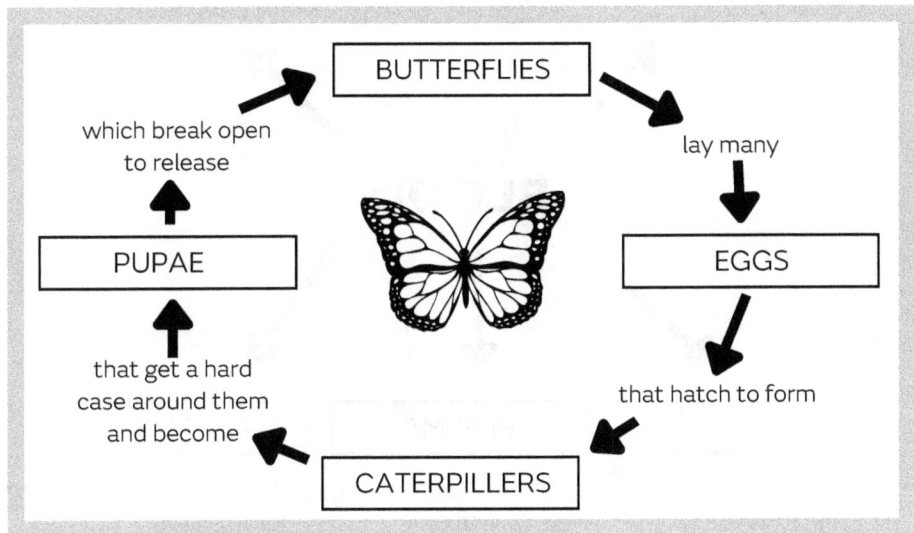

RADIAL MAPS

These maps are used when a reading has a main topic with details given of its smaller aspects or sub-topics. The topic is shown in a central box with key terms and brief notes on them in surrounding boxes at the end of radial spokes.

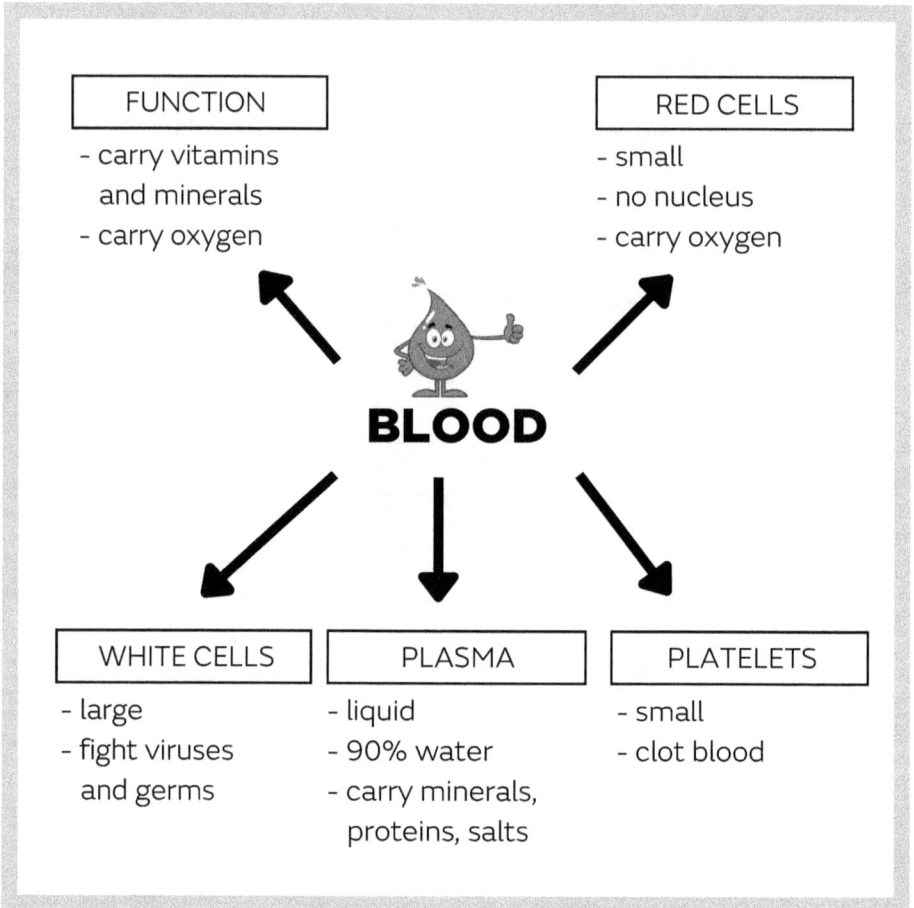

FUNCTION		RED CELLS
- carry vitamins and minerals - carry oxygen		- small - no nucleus - carry oxygen

BLOOD

WHITE CELLS	PLASMA	PLATELETS
- large - fight viruses and germs	- liquid - 90% water - carry minerals, proteins, salts	- small - clot blood

CONVERGING MAPS

These maps are used to summarise the causes that lead to an effect. The maps are often called fishbone maps because of their shape as you will see in the example below.

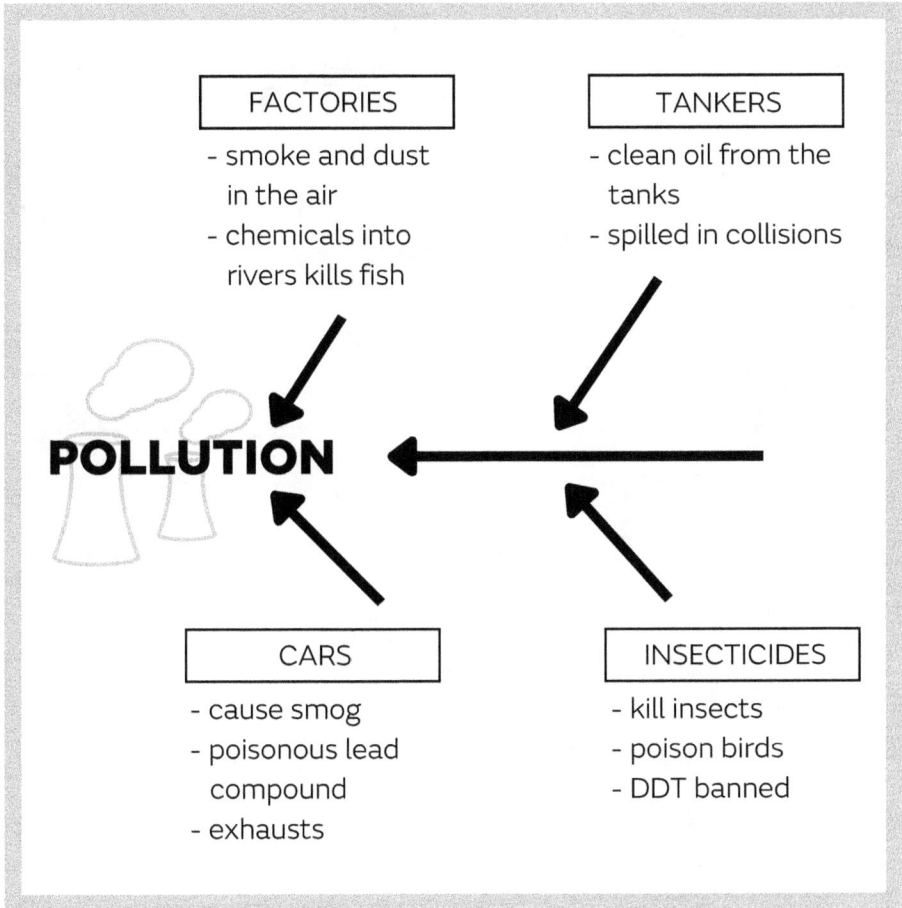

FACTORIES
- smoke and dust in the air
- chemicals into rivers kills fish

TANKERS
- clean oil from the tanks
- spilled in collisions

POLLUTION

CARS
- cause smog
- poisonous lead compound
- exhausts

INSECTICIDES
- kill insects
- poison birds
- DDT banned

COMPARISON MAPS

These maps are used to show how two things are both similar and different. They are made up of two overlapping circles or three columns.

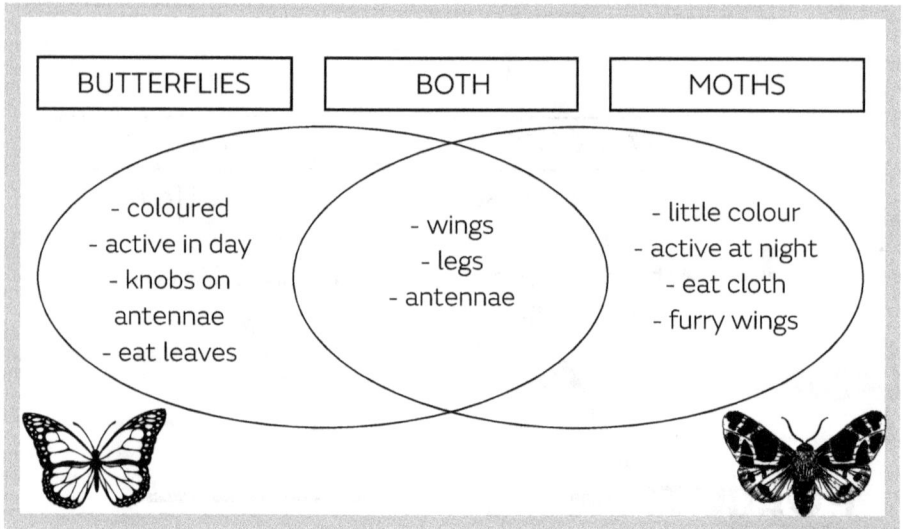

BUTTERFLIES	BOTH	MOTHS

- coloured
- active in day
- knobs on antennae
- eat leaves

- wings
- legs
- antennae

- little colour
- active at night
- eat cloth
- furry wings

HIERARCHICAL MAPS

These maps are used when a main topic is broken down into smaller and smaller topics and sub-topics. Each sub-topic is part of a larger topic. The terms are put in boxes with a few connecting words along arrows to show how the terms are related.

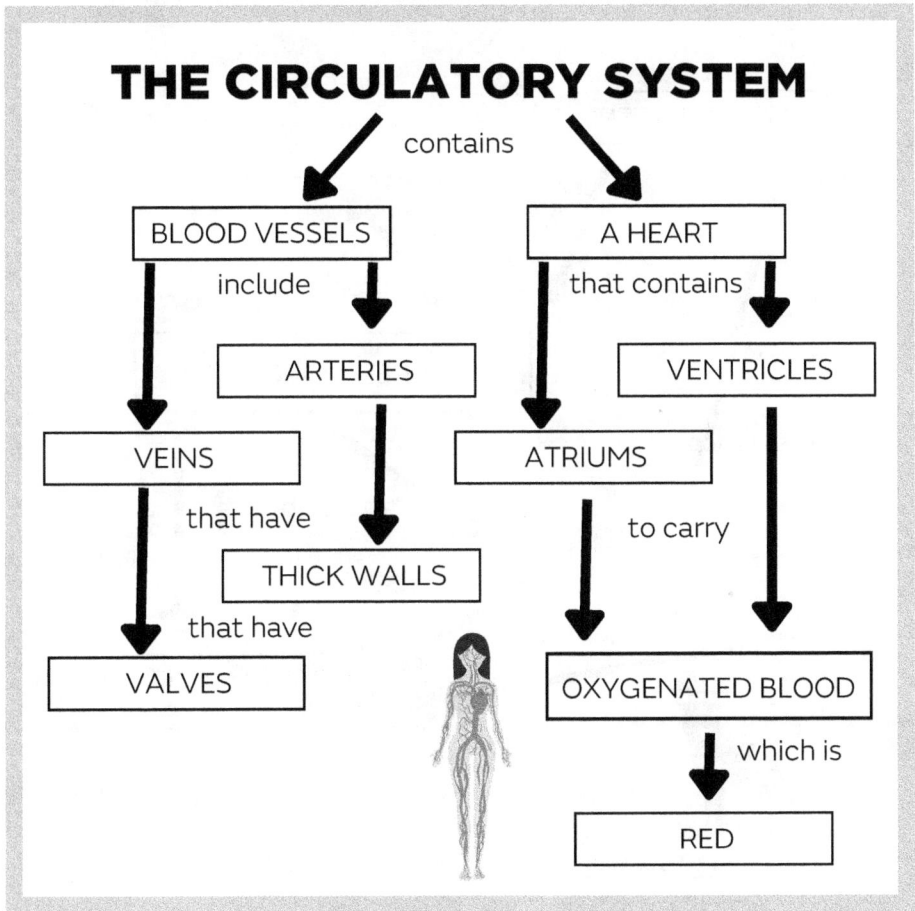

THE CIRCULATORY SYSTEM

contains

```
BLOOD VESSELS                          A HEART
     include                              that contains
              ARTERIES                            VENTRICLES

VEINS                        ATRIUMS

     that have                   to carry
              THICK WALLS

     that have
VALVES                                   OXYGENATED BLOOD

                                              which is
                                                   RED
```

INTERACTING MAPS

These maps are used to show how different people or things interact with each other. The example below creates a map using a well-known fairytale.

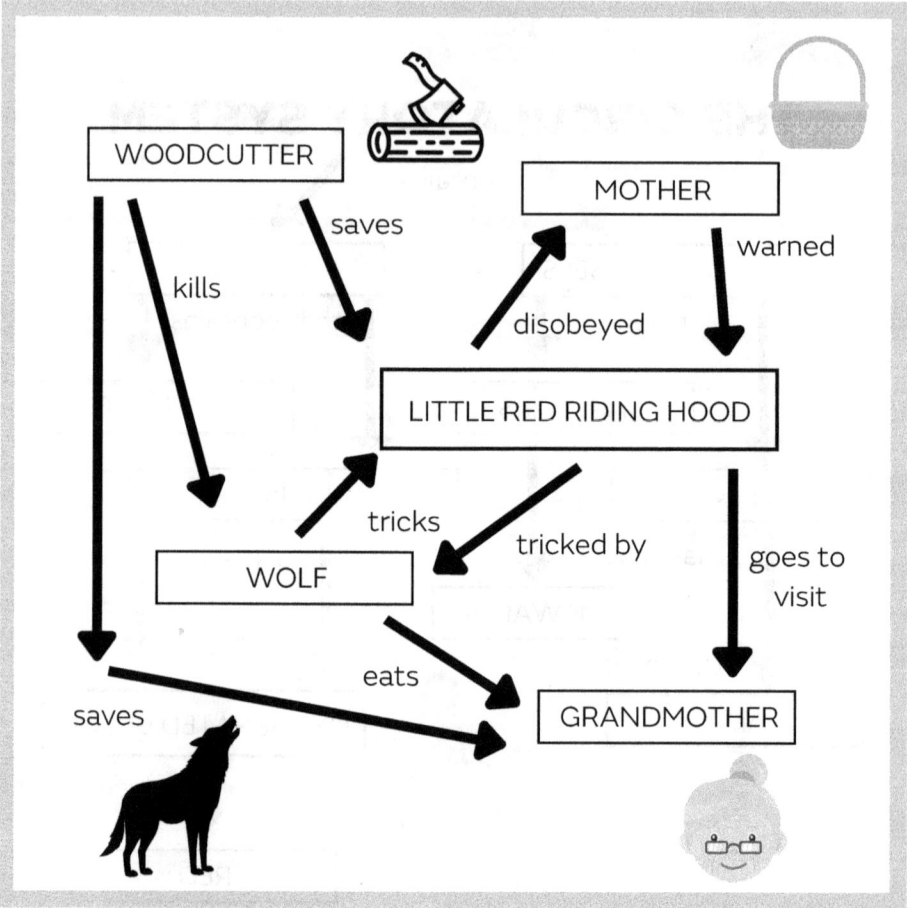

WOODCUTTER

MOTHER

LITTLE RED RIDING HOOD

WOLF

GRANDMOTHER

saves

kills

warned

disobeyed

tricks

tricked by

goes to visit

eats

saves

COMPARISON MAPS FOR THREE OR MORE THINGS

These maps are used to compare three or more things. Examples are shown along one axis and properties along the other.

SOLID	CONDUCTS ELECTRICITY	MELTING POINT	MAGNETIC
Iron	Yes	High	Yes
Plastic	No	Low	No
Copper	No	High	No
Glass	No	High	No

LINEAR MAPS

These maps are used to show the stages of a step-at-a-time process that has a definite start and finish.

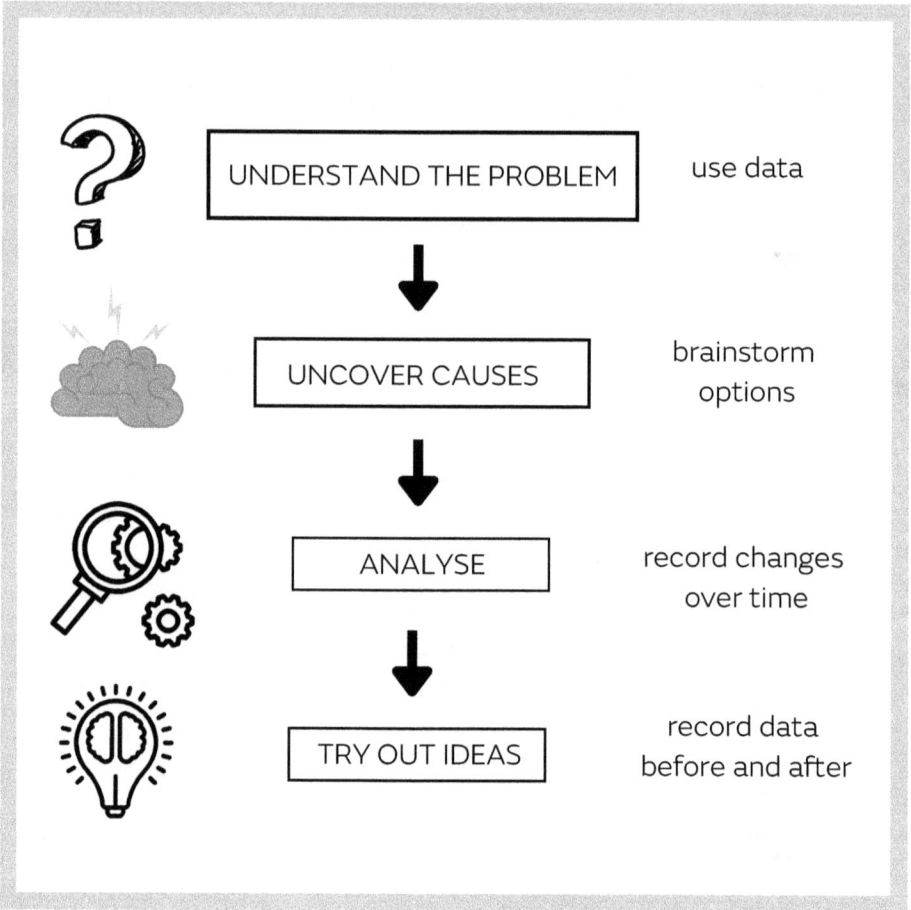

UNDERSTAND THE PROBLEM   use data

UNCOVER CAUSES   brainstorm options

ANALYSE   record changes over time

TRY OUT IDEAS   record data before and after

VISUAL SUMMARISING

Now that we have seen the shape and details of some standard maps, let's list the key steps involved in visually summarising a reading or presentation.

1. Be aware of a range of standard shapes that are used for visual summarising.

2. Understand the kind of information that each map is good for understanding.

3. Identify ten or more key words on each page of a reading, article or extract of a talk. These words should be fairly specific and be what most people would associate with the topic under discussion. They may be complex words, or words that are repeated in the reading, or even words that are unknown to you. This is not an easy task. The key words chosen may vary widely from person to person.

4. Find some groups of words that are connected to each other and think about how to connect them geometrically on a diagram. To do this, ask some questions such as:

    ♦ Are two or more things being compared here?
    ♦ Are there some parts or stages here that are part of a cyclic or linear process?
    ♦ Is there a main topic that is being broken down into smaller and smaller sub-topics?
    ♦ Are different aspects of a main topic being discussed?
    ♦ Are there some causes being discussed that lead to an effect?
    ♦ Are actions or feelings between people being discussed here?

5. Select one or more map for summarising groups of key words.

6. On each map, write in the key words, together with one to five words between each pair that show the connection between them. When different aspects, or the causes, of a topic are being described a few notes or sub-headings will be more appropriate than connections.

Activity

Read the information in the newspaper article. As you do, try to identify some standard visual maps that can be used to summarise the main terms and their connections. Get someone else to visually summarise this reading on some standard maps. There is no one correct way of doing this task.

THE GREEN NEWS

Plants make oxygen, which is breathed in by humans and other animals. The animals breathe out carbon dioxide, which is taken in by plants so that they can make their own food in order to grow. Plants also use water and chemicals from the soil and light energy from the sun to make food from the carbon dioxide. Chemicals are returned to the soil when animals and plants die.

Different kinds of plants grow in different regions of the Earth. The plants on mountains differ from those in tropical forests, deserts, swamps, coastlines and the sea.

Flowering plants have roots, stems, leaves and flowers. Roots hold the plant firmly in the ground and take up water and chemicals from the soil.

Stems hold the leaves and flowers and lift them up so that they can receive plenty of sunlight.

Leaves are the food factory of the plant. Their green chemical, called chlorophyll, unites the water, carbon dioxide and light to form starch. Starch makes the stems of plants grow.

Flowers are the reproductive parts of plants. They contain the male stamens and the female pistils. Pollen grains from a stamen fertilise the egg in a pistil to form a seed.

Humans have killed many types of plants, but now we are trying to conserve those plants which have very few numbers left on the Earth, particularly the plants of rainforests.

GRAPHIC ORGANISERS

Here are some graphic organisers which help draw a clear picture of some of the key terms, and their connections, from the article on the previous page. Keep the words to a minimum as the organiser aims to remove the clutter and highlight the key words and their connections.

Cyclical Map Showing Stages

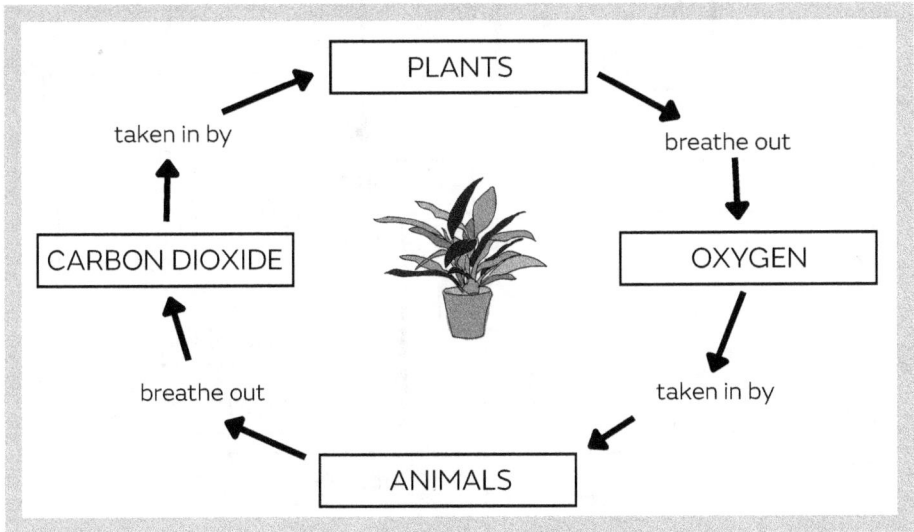

Radial Map Showing Key Aspects Discussed

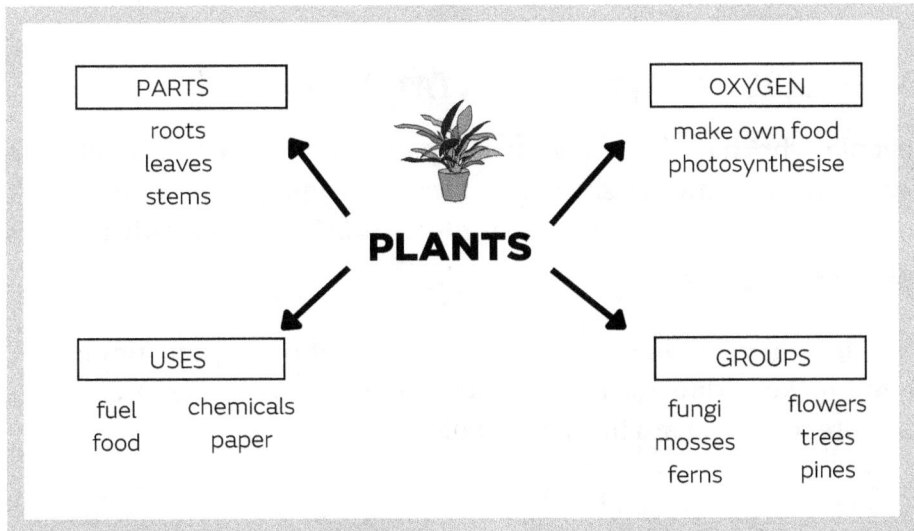

FLOWERING PLANTS

have

ROOTS   FLOWERS   LEAVES

for taking in   for supporting   that contain   that contain   that contain

TRUNKS

CHLOROPHYLL

WATER

PISTILS

that unites with sunlight

from the

that form

STAMENS

WATER

that release

CARBON DIOXIDE

SOIL

SEEDS

to form

POLLEN GRAINS

STARCH

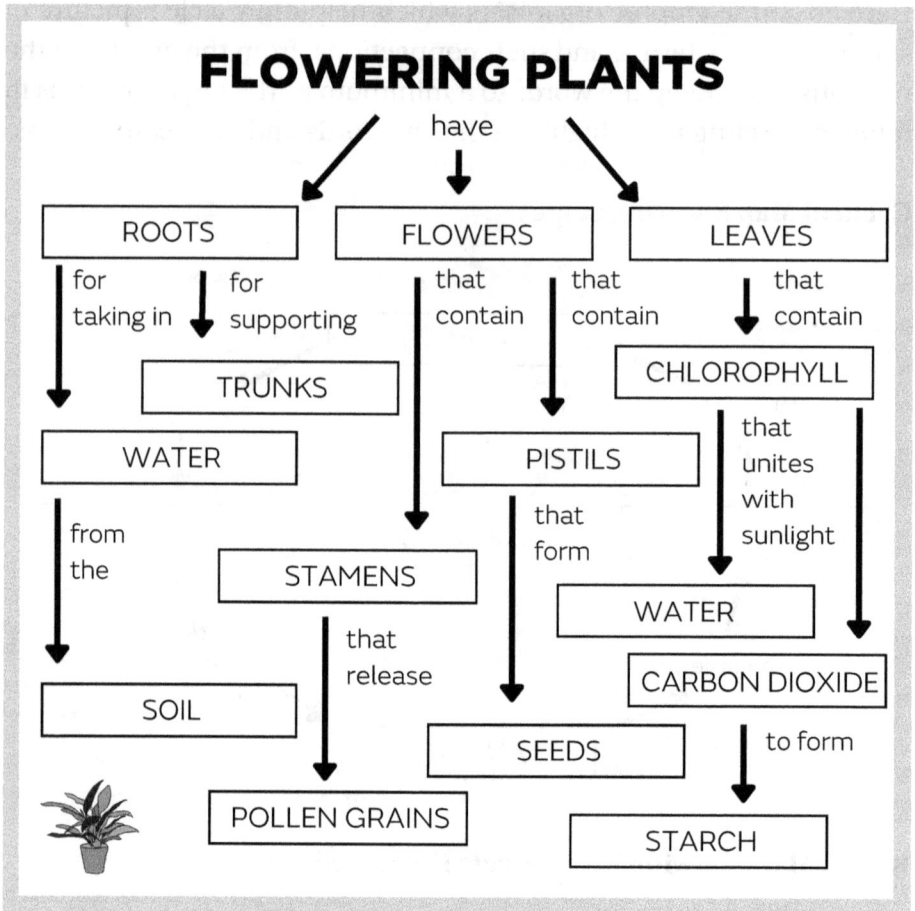

VISUALISING WITH MENTAL MAPS

People who have a strong visual-spatial intelligence naturally use 'doodles' or thumbnail sketches to record the images they have in their minds. They find it easier to summarise information with pictures rather than words.

Because they are linear and sequential in nature, verbal summaries. often make it difficult to 'see' inter-relationships between concepts that are read or heard in a presentation.

If you find visualising difficult, start using symbols, shapes, colour and arrows to summarise your thinking. It takes practice to identify and represent the key words and ideas in information and how they fit together.

Mental maps are good for organising as well as summarising. They assist in planning a report or piece of creative writing. They also enable you to get inside the mind of students and workers to see the kinds of pictures they have in their memories. When you ask people to draw a map on a particular topic, it is very easy to identify misconnections they have between ideas and key words. These misconceptions need to be cleared up, before developing new aspects of the topic.

We all imagine, or visualise, things in different ways; even a common piece of information. It is interesting to ask people to visually summarise the same page or two of information. The range of maps, in terms of their shape and detail, will amaze you!

Later, in Chapter 10 on improving your memory, mention is made of the technique of deep processing. Here again you will be amazed at the range of mental images different people have for, say, a common story. Some people construct a very vivid picture of events, often in colour, and which involves movement, noises, smells, and even tastes. Other people find it difficult to draw any mental picture at all.

Learning to draw better mental maps is a vital skill towards helping you develop any intelligence. If you can't draw a clear physical map on paper then there is little hope of you drawing one in your memory. Fuzzy, confused mental pictures are not helpful if we want to think more intelligently.

KEY POINTS

☑ Good thinkers are good at mentally picturing a summary of information they hear or see.

☑ Mental maps can be drawn on paper, which are often called graphic organisers.

☑ Asking students to design their own questions for some given content helps them to better understand the content and the processes involved. Graphic organisers clarify and summarise the key terms in information and the way these terms are connected to each other.

☑ The key terms in a reading are usually related to each other in one of a few standard geometric shapes or graphic organisers.

☑ The shape of the graphic organiser chosen is the same as the shape of the information it summarises.

☑ Research shows that the use of graphic organisers helps learners to both increase their recall and understanding of information they see and hear.

CHAPTER 7

CREATIVE THINKING

Pre-reading questions to ponder:

- ◆ What is creative thinking?
- ◆ How can we test for creative thought?
- ◆ What are some blocks to creative thinking?
- ◆ Why do some people find it difficult to think creatively?
- ◆ What are some teachable strategies for improving creative thought?

Young students are good at flexible thinking because they fantasise, they improvise and they are inventive in their play. On the other hand, older students show little growth in their flexible thinking. This is because older students soon learn at school that they get rewards for the correct answer they have been taught, and not a different one. Questions with only one correct answer demand convergent or correct answer thinking, whereas questions that invite a range of 'correct' answers encourage flexible or creative thought. Consequently, most people need to be taught some strategies for 'breaking away' in order to regain their former ability to mentally flex.

Let's begin by checking what you are like at creative thinking. Try this simple activity.

Activity

Place your pencil point on the dot under A.

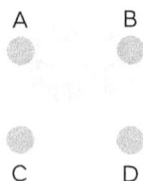

A   B

C   D

Now use only 3 **straight** lines to join the dots A to B, B to D, D to C and C to A. The end of one line should join the start of the following line it touches.

Did you say that it should be four, and not three straight lines? A to B is one line, B to D is two, D to C is three, and C to A is four! This is a reasonable thought because your brain sees the four points A, B, C, and D as being at the corners of a square. You have seen plenty of squares. And your brain, which is a wonderful recogniser and storer of common patterns, remembers that a square needs four lines joining its points together.

As previously mentioned, the brain's incredible ability to remember, and stick with patterns it sees regularly, is the reason why some people find it difficult to think creatively. The brains of such people make it difficult for them to 'break away', or escape, from the patterns they have remembered. Here is a key point to remember.

You need to try hard to escape or break away from usual or common patterns stored in your memory if you want to think creatively.

Getting back to the activity. When you draw the line from A to B you need to escape the pattern of a square in your memory. So, when you get to B you need to keep going straight ahead for about the same length as A to B. Now, draw your second line down from the end of this first line through D and stop when you are below the points C and A. Finally, draw your third line up through C to A. Three lines! Notice that to come up with this creative solution you had to break away from a usual pattern. At the point B, you had to think flexibly, or in other words, creatively.

Let's try another task to see if you are loosening up. This is a common task asked in tests of creative thinking. Try it on a piece of scrap paper.

Activity

In 3 minutes, write down all of the unusual uses you can think of for a brick.

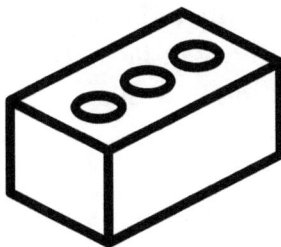

You can give marks for the ideas you come up with in one of several ways. For example:

1. One mark for **each idea you come up with that is acceptable** to most people. Most people wouldn't agree with you if you suggested a brick could be used to build a boat or as a pillow! (The number of ideas is called **FLUENCY OF IDEAS.**)

2. One mark for **each idea that only you come up with** compared with those of other people in a class, family, or other group that is also doing the test. If you were the only one in a group to suggest that a brick could be used as a door stop or as a pencil holder then you receive one mark for each of these unique ideas. (Here we are marking for **UNIQUENESS OF IDEAS.**)

3. One mark for **each different category of ideas** you come up with that is acceptable to most people. For example, to use a brick as a hammer or as a paper-weight are two different categories of ideas and deserve one mark for each. But to use a brick to build a wall, to build a church, or to build a house, are examples within the same category of 'for building a vertical structure'. Hence, there is only one point for this category even though three examples were given. (The number of different categories/groups of ideas is called **FLEXIBILITY OF IDEAS.**)

Research shows that Method Three, marking the number of different categories of ideas given (flexibility of thinking) is the best measure of creative thinking. Fluency of ideas (Method One) correlates too strongly with, or is too closely dependent on, a person's verbal ability and memory of facts. Uniqueness of ideas is also poor because this depends on how many people there are in the group doing the test for creativity.

Flexibility of ideas is least related to correct answer thinking, and obviously is the best measure of a person's ability to 'shift mental gears' or to break away from usual patterns of thinking. This is how we will score your answers to the test item. Here are some suggested categories of ideas. Remember, one point is allocated for each of these categories but not for each example within these categories.

Vertical structure
Horizontal structure
Weapon
Weight
Support
Border
Tool
Wedge
To sit or stand on
To carve
A holder for pens/flowers
A ruler/stencil
Chalk
Abrasive
Ramp
Home for insects
Fill up space
To lift/balance
(others possible)

From my observations a score of about three to five categories is average. However, if you come up with a score of seven or more different categories you are in the top three to five per cent of people in most age groups. That is right, even eight-year-olds can think as flexibly as older students. There is little growth of creative thinking with age. This is different from convergent, or correct answer, thinking which naturally increases with age as our knowledge and life experiences increase.

OTHER WAYS OF IDENTIFYING CREATIVITY

The Langrehr Test of Creative Thinking (see Appendix B) is one of many cognitive skills tests for measuring creativity. This type of test is still the most popular, despite the criticisms that little knowledge of content is needed and that there is a degree of subjectivity in deciding what are acceptable answers.

Personality inventories are also sometimes used. Here an observer rates a person on a list of characteristics that are associated with well-known creative people. These characteristics include:

Curiosity
Uninhibited
High risk taker
Intellectually playful
Sense of humour
Emotional sensitivity
Sense of beauty
Unwillingness to accept authority
Tolerance of ambiguity
Perseverance
Openness to new experiences
Independence.

Then there are parent/teacher/peer ratings of who they think are creative. These ratings are subject to a 'halo' or favourite effect. Art scales, that consider the preferences an individual has for a picture in a pair of pictures, have also been used. These preferences are then compared with the preferences of highly creative people.

It is not enough to claim high creativity based on a pencil and paper test, although such tests do identify the ability to flex and break away from usual ways of thinking. A well-known definition of creativity is, 'the ability to produce work that is both novel and appropriate.' But what is novel and what is appropriate?

This is where the subjectivity of identifying creativity comes in. 'Novel' suggests original, unpredictable, and provoking surprise. While 'appropriate' suggests sensible and useful. And then there is the question, 'Can you be creative when writing poetry but not when writing stories or drawing designs?' Assessing creativity obviously depends on the audience, the judge, and the skill being assessed.

BLOCKS TO CREATIVE THINKING

Relax, we can all think creatively to some degree. If you have found creative thought difficult before, it doesn't follow that you are not intelligent. In fact, there is only a weak relationship between correct answer thinking and thinking that involves flexibility of thought. There are obviously a variety of blocks that make it difficult for intelligent people to break away from correct answer or dominant pattern thinking in order to think creatively. These blocks that limit our thinking relate to our personality and to our style of thinking.

Personality as a block

Personality and a method of assessing its dimensions is discussed in Chapter 9. Some dimensions of personality lend themselves to flexible and creative thinking more than others. After having read Chapter 9, if you think you are an N more than a S, and a P more than a J, then you have a personality for helping creative thought. Unfortunately, a majority of teachers have a SJ temperament type! If this is you then it is important to learn some of the strategies discussed in this chapter.

Thinking style as a block

Researchers have suggested many different thinking styles that we use to perceive and make sense of information around us. Perhaps the most relevant is a style called field dependence-field independence. This is discussed in Chapter 9. You will be able to try a test item for this style of thinking in this later chapter.

After reading Chapter 9, I think you will agree that field dependent people find it easier to think creatively.

Socially acceptable behaviour as a block

As well as our personality and our thinking style, the norms of acceptable social and emotional behaviour limit our ability to think creatively. Have a look at the table below. How many of the blocks apply to you?

BLOCKS TO CREATIVE THINKING

Our **inability** to....

1. Sleep on ideas. Most people need things finished and out of the way as quickly as possible. Many creative ideas only come forward after many days or weeks of incubation.

2. Offer a possibly incorrect suggestion in front of a group. Most people feel more comfortable criticising ideas rather than creating them. They have learnt that it is bad to make mistakes because they may be ridiculed by the group.

3. Live with chaos or ambiguity. Creativity often comes out of a messy arrangement of bits and pieces of things or data rather than neat and tidy arrangements.

4. Fantasise or daydream. We learn that this is only for young children. However, some very creative ideas come forward at first light when you are half asleep. Some also come when you are very relaxed, out on a walk or are almost dreaming in front of a fire. And some come while you are under a shower.

5. Do socially unacceptable things. Would you bend a coin, or tear up a playing card, in order to creatively solve a problem?

6. Escape from stereotypes or traditional roles and combinations.

7. Observe specific details in the designs and structures that we 'see' each day. We are so bombarded with visual information that we become visually saturated. Do you know what all the buttons on your car do or what is on the cover of your latest novel?

8. Escape from usual geometric patterns. We are often trapped within their boundaries.

I know it is difficult to change your personality and temperament in order to help you become more creative in your thinking. However, if you keep in mind the blocks above, and learn some of the freeing strategies in the next section, you will give yourself the best chance for thinking creatively.

If you have a favourable thinking style and temperament for creative thinking you still need to have a positive attitude. Good thinkers are good at the four Ps of the thinking process. In other words, they are good at recognising patterns in the information they attend to, they have a positive attitude that helps them attend, they ask themselves probing questions, and they clarify and summarise information with mental pictures. The important thing here is that creative thinkers have a distinct positive attitude that you can keep in mind.

Creative thinking requires the right kind of attitude. Make sure it is a positive one. Remember the acronym FIRST!

THE POSITIVITY OF CREATIVE THINKERS: FIRST

F	Creative thinkers '**fantasise**'. They try out way-out ideas, they try the unusual, and even the impossible.
I	Creative thinkers '**incubate**' or sit on ideas. They don't rush in and accept the first answer or solution they think of. Often the second or third idea is the most creative one.
R	Creative thinkers are '**risk takers**'. They don't mind people laughing at their suggestions. In fact, they enjoy people laughing at their way-out ideas.
S	Creative thinkers are '**sensitive**' to the creativity about them. They notice and question the design of the creative forms of nature and those created by human beings.
T	Creative thinkers '**titillate**' or have fun with ideas. Some people say that creative thinking is aided by 'happy molecules' or endorphins that are created in the brain when we are happy or relaxed. Endorphins are usually in high concentration in the brain when we first wake in the morning or later, under the shower, as we listen to the water fall.

THE PROBING OF CREATIVE THINKING

What kinds of probing questions pass through the minds of creative thinkers as they design or solve problems? If you remember another acronym, CREATE, it will remind you of six of them.

Remember CREATE

C	Can I '**combine**' some things together?
R	Can I use '**random input**' or '**reverse**' some parts or processes here?
E	Can I '**eliminate**' or remove some part or process?
A	Can I use '**alternative**' methods or materials?
T	Can I '**twist**' things around a bit?
E	Can I '**elaborate**' or add something?

Did you notice that most of these words suggest 'breaking away', or trying something novel and different?

APPLYING CREATE

Keep CREATE in mind. Below is an activity to see how well you can break away from a traditional design that you look at every morning. It is the design of a box of breakfast cereal.

Activity

Come up with some fresh ideas for changing the design of a box of breakfast cereal in order to make it more interesting, creative, and useful. Write down your ideas.

Did CREATE help you? Here are a few of my thoughts.

C: Stands for *combine*. Maybe combine the cereal pieces into bite size chunks. Maybe combine some powdered milk with the cereal so that all we have to do is add water.

R: Stands for **random input**. How about flowers as some random input? Some attributes of flowers include: they are scented, have different colours, shapes and seeds. Maybe some rose or violet scented cereal, cereal pieces in the shapes and colours of flowers, packets of flower seeds in the box, flower pictures on the box.

E: Stands for **eliminate**. Why not eliminate the cardboard box and have a printed, see-through plastic bag?

A: Stands for **alternatives**. Rather than cardboard for the box, use a material that can be fed to the dog.

T: Stands for **twists** or reversals. Why not open the box at the side instead of the top?

E: Stands for **elaborate** or **extend** the design. How about building a pourer into the top of the box? E also stands for **extreme cases**. Design a very large or very small box of cereal ... it may be useful.

There are strategies such as forced combinations, random input, attribute listing, attribute analysis, and reverse questioning, that can all help us to break away from traditional patterns in our memories. Let's have a closer look at these strategies.

'C' FOR FORCING COMBINATIONS

Many new products have been created by combining two or more quite unrelated objects. For example, a clock and a radio, a watch and a calculator, or a home and a trailer.

Activity

What potentially new garden tool can you create by combining any two of the following tools?

A hose	A rake	A spade	A broom
A saw	A pick	A crowbar	A barrow

How about a broom with a hollow handle and end attachment for a hose to squirt water down the inside of the handle?

A New Wardrobe

New products are also created by listing the choices that are available within each part of a product. Many new products become available by combining one choice from each part with choices from each of the other parts. Fill in some choices for each of the parts of a shirt shown on the table below.

	Sleeves	Material	Pattern	Method of Fastening
1.	Long	Cotton	Stripes	Zipper
2.				
3.				
4.				

How many potentially different shirts can be created?

A New Method of Transport

For those of us more into cars and other vehicles, what new form of transport can we create from these choices within the parts listed?

Body Material	Power Source	Operating Material
Plastic	Petrol	Roads
Fibreglass	Alchohol	Rails
Steel	Solar	Mono Rail
Aluminium	Electricity	Water
Wood	Magnetism	Air

What about a solar powered, fibreglass craft that moves on water?

Imagine the combinations that may not have become obvious without listing choices within their attributes in this way.

'R' FOR RANDOM INPUT

Random input is a useful strategy for coming up with quite unexpected solutions to a problem, or changes to the design of a product. A random input is an object that is chosen before you have knowledge of a problem to solve or a product to change. I repeat, it should not be linked with the problem or product in any way.

First, select the random input and list some of its attributes or properties. Next, try to use some of these attributes to generate some potential ideas. If no fresh ideas come up, try some new random input.

Activity

Random input - newspaper (my choice)

Attributes of input (list some for a newspaper)

Object to improve - toothbrush

Potential solutions. (Try to make some creative links between the attributes of the newspaper and some new design of a toothbrush.)

Did you come up with any unexpected ideas? You never know, they might make you your first million dollars. Here are some of my attributes for the random input: large area, printed, flexible, separate pieces, soft, light, and porous.

My potential improvements to the design of the toothbrush are:

- Separate or replaceable brushes to fit on the handle.
- A flexible or pivoted brush.
- Printed personal names on the handle.
- A large area brush to clean both rows of teeth at once.

Now, how about using random input for a little creative problem solving? I'll state a problem and choose the random input. You list some attributes and then try to use them to suggest some unexpected and possibly crazy solutions.

Activity

Random input - book

Problem - traffic congestion in city streets

My attributes for the book were: pages, numbers, sections, spine, index, title, and library.

Now for a potential solution. Maybe number the streets, with one way traffic down odd numbered streets and in the opposite direction down even numbered streets. Busy sections of the city could be continually broadcast on a city radio frequency.

'E' FOR ELIMINATE

The idea here is to challenge the necessity of the number of parts or processes involved with something that you use or do each day. Are there any parts that could possibly be eliminated to create a product of better design? This is how someone came up with the idea of eliminating tubes from car tyres, coins from phone boxes, spokes from motorcycle wheels, and so on.

'A' IS FOR ALTERNATIVES AND ATTRIBUTE LISTING

You have just seen how listing attributes of random input can help you to come up with unexpected or unplanned improvements to products and solutions to problems. Attribute listing by itself can be done with any object in order to come up with some alternative uses for it.

Remember the item for testing your flexibility of thinking? Let's try a new object, such as a newspaper, to find some different uses for it. List some attributes in the first column and in the next column list some things or tasks that use each of these attributes.

	Newspaper Attributes	Tasks that Need this Attribute
1.	Porous	Cleaning windows, soaking up liquids
2.		
3.		

Some of my attributes included porous, like window cleaning cloths, and light/crumbles easily, which makes it ideal for packing breakables. It has a large area so is good for covering floors, walls and books, and for shading things from the sun. It tears and rots easily, which makes it useful for garden mulch. It is also lightweight and so it makes good kites. Further, it is thin and burns easily, and so on.

'T' FOR TWISTING

Look for opportunities to place something up rather than down, to the back rather than the front, outwards rather than inwards, or sideways rather than straight forward. Simply, be prepared to break away from usual placements. You never know when it might be useful to catch and store rain water in an upside down umbrella rather than using it to keep the rain off you!

'E' IS FOR ELABORATE OR EXTREME CASES

I use the acronym SCUMPS to think about extreme cases of an object.

- What would be the use of an extremely small or large example of this creation?
- Would there be a use for a black, white, or iridescent form of this creation?
- What could this object be made of?
- How useful would a rubber one of these be?

Next is an activity that requires you to consider some elaborate and extreme cases.

Activity

Can you write down a use for each of the following:

1. A very large pencil?

2. A very small comb?

3. An iridescent cup?

4. A very soft brick?

5. A mug with two handles?

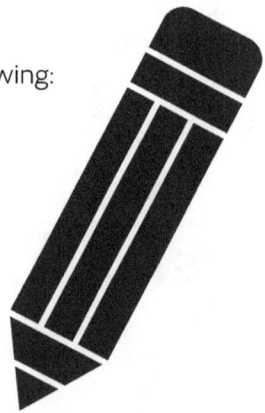

Possible answers are:

1. Large pencils for marking out-of-reach spots, for people with big hands or who wear pencils out quickly or who lose them easily.

2. Very small combs for moustaches, for eyebrows, for men with little hair.

3. A cup for middle of the night drinking or for campers.

4. A soft brick to throw in plays and at the TV when you are cross.

5. A two-handled mug for more control when drinking hot soup!

Elaboration involves building on, or extending, an idea. Talking of building, it is fun to use your creative thoughts to design and build structures, given some limits. For example, you might like to try the following in competition with some friends:

Activity

Build the tallest free-standing structure that you can using only 30 matches and a stick of plasticine.

Build a structure that will support a selected book, 2 centimetres above a table top, using only a sheet of A4 paper and some sticky tape.

'D' IS FOR DISADVANTAGES

D isn't in our acronym CREATE. Never mind, D stands for disadvantages in the design of a creative product. Listing these negatives can help you to focus on possible changes for a new creation.

Activity

What changes would you make to the design of a:

1. Car tyre so that it will last longer?

2. Pair of glasses so they don't irritate your nose as much?

Maybe, tyres with metal or hardened plastic in the rubber. And glasses that hang down from a head band or with foam on the bridge.

You all have the potential to break away from those patterns that your brain locks you into. Try some of these strategies and you will be amazed at how your thinking will become ever so much more flexible and imaginative.

GROUP STRATEGIES FOR GENERATING CREATIVE IDEAS

Dozens of methods have been suggested for this type of problem. solving. Here is a condensed version of three of them.

Method 5:5:3

Five people sit in a circular group. Each person has 5 minutes to write down on a piece of paper up to 3 ideas for solving a problem.

The papers are given to each group facilitator who numbers the ideas 1 to 15 and reads them out 1 at a time. Individuals in each group rate each idea as they are read out:

5 = excellent
3 = good
1 = average

The total rating points for each idea are summed by the group facilitator at the end. The 3 highest rating ideas are presented to the large group for discussion and evaluation.

Ranking the Top 3

Groups of less than 10 people are formed. Individuals write an idea on paper and pin it up (gallery method) or place it in a pool (pool method) for all to see. Individuals generate a second idea for pooling or display. Individuals rank the best 3 ideas pooled or displayed.

Best idea ranks a 1, second best a 2, and third best a 3. Total rankings awarded by individuals to each idea on display, or pooled, are calculated by the group facilitator.

The 3 best ideas (lowest ranking points) are presented to the larger group for evaluation.

Combining Ideas

There are 4 to 6 people per group. Each person spends 5 minutes listing some ideas. Now, each person writes their best idea on a piece of paper and places it in a group pool for all in the group to see.

The group tries to combine 2 or more ideas to form an 'add-on idea'.

THE BEST TIME FOR CREATIVE THINKING

When are our brains ready to flex and ready to let us break away from the usual patterns it stores for us? The answer is when they are relaxed and 'happy'. Apparently, in this state the brain produces plenty of chemicals called endorphins that it needs to generate new ideas. And in this state it has plenty of theta brain waves that also help us to dream up unusual ideas and solutions.

The ideal time for endorphins and theta wave activity would be the first thing in the morning as you are just waking. It could also be later under the shower as the water trickles down to relax you. Or it could be just as you are about to nod off to sleep. Many inventors have had their best ideas just as they were going to sleep. Overall, it is important to be free of stress and to be playful with the ideas you are working on.

KEY POINTS

☑ Creative thinking will enhance any of your intelligences because it enables you to escape from usual ways, or patterns, of doing, making, or thinking about things in general.

☑ Your personality and temperament play a big part in controlling your ability to take risks and to fantasise. Low risk-takers need strategies to help them to break away.

☑ Creative thinking is most likely when you are almost semi-conscious, with the brain being relaxed and generating plenty of theta waves.

☑ The strategies used to encourage creative thinking can be learned and have been shown to increase flexibility of thought.

CHAPTER 8

CRITICAL THINKING

Pre-reading questions to ponder:

- ◆ What is critical thinking?
- ◆ What kind of positive attitude is needed for strong critical thinking?
- ◆ What kinds of questions do strong critical thinkers ask themselves?
- ◆ What kinds of core thinking processes relate to critical thinking?

Critical thinking and creative thinking are probably the most important, and yet the most neglected, forms of thinking needed in our rapidly changing world. Having a good memory for prescribed facts no longer guarantees success in life after school. And yet schools and universities do little to help students to develop these higher forms of thinking. This could be due to the fact that it is difficult to assess critical and creative thinking with pencil and paper tests. However, some university departments, such as medical schools design tests of these forms of thinking as part of their entrance selection process.

WHAT IS CRITICAL THINKING?

Critical thinking is the process of judging information, with the aid of relevant criteria.

For example, we can judge the relevance, reliability, consistency, accuracy, bias, and so on, of most information. However, most people don't bother to think critically when they read or hear information. They read the content and ideas and accept them as being accurate, reliable, and unbiased because they have been published in a book, magazine or online newspaper.

Possibly the one time when we really try to think critically is during a debate or argument about an issue that emotionally involves us. Here, we tend to dig deep for evidence, examples, criteria, and clear, logical thought.

We need more people who can think and challenge what they read and hear. We need more strong critical thinkers!

POSITIVITY OF CRITICAL THINKERS

Did you notice the phrase 'strong critical thinkers' in the sentence before? Well, who or what are weak critical thinkers? These are people who argue or judge information in a negative or destructive way.

Weak critical thinkers lack the necessary fairness, objectivity and flexibility to make proper judgements about information. And they lack the relevant criteria and probing questions needed to evaluate it. Well, what kind of positivity or attitude does a strong critical thinker have when judging information? I remember some of the features with the acronym COOL! It is different from FIRST, the acronym I suggested for the positivity needed for creative thinking.

APPLYING COOL

C	The critical thinker tries to '**clarify**' what it is he or she is judging, what is the main idea being argued about, what do we already know about the issue, what is the meaning of key terms, what is the other side to this issue, and so on. Many people debate or evaluate an issue without being clear about these things.
O	Critical thinkers are '**open-minded**' and fair-minded. That is, they think dialogically rather than monologically. Most people in a debate only consider their own point of view. I am right, you are wrong! I don't want to hear why you think the opposite to me! This black or white monological thinking can be egocentric or socio-centric. We need to learn to be fair-minded and at least listen to the other person's point of view. Listen to his or her reasons. We have to help young people to be open-minded because the reason behind interpersonal or international conflicts today is the lack of open-mindedness.

O	Critical thinkers are '**objective**' rather than subjective in their judgements. That is, they consider all the facts, the data, the examples, the statistics and the evidence, before making their judgement of information. Weak critical thinkers make emotional judgements based on feelings or hunches that are not supported by evidence or the facts. In other words, they are subjective in making their judgements.
L	Critical thinkers are '**loose**' or flexible. I chose L to make up a simple acronym COOL! Anyhow, the critical thinker is prepared to modify his or her position when presented with new information. Don't be pig-headed. Get the complete picture.

PATTERNS SENSED BY CRITICAL THINKERS

Creative thinkers tend to sense patterns in features such as the shape, size, colour, texture, balance, simplicity and emphasis of visual and tactual things. On the other hand, critical thinkers look for weaknesses in the patterns of spoken and written words that make up ideas, stated claims, examples given, evidence stated, feelings and opinions expressed. Let's look at some of the probing questions that critical thinkers ask themselves when considering these patterns. These enable them to identify such things as bias, irrelevance, over-generalisation, unreliability, lack of evidence, inconsistency, and so on.

PROBING QUESTIONS FOR CRITICAL THINKING

What kind of probing or self-questioning goes on inside the mind of a strong critical thinker as they judge some information? First, let's check the kinds of questions that pass through your mind as you try to make judgements about the letter to a newspaper below on the topic of daylight saving.

When daylight saving came to an end once more a few weeks ago, we could almost hear the sigh of relief from the vast majority of citizens.

Yes, I know that 16 years ago a sizeable majority voted in favour of introducing this ridiculous interference with our timekeeping. Now we have learnt from bitter experience how many problems it has created.

I acknowledge that there are still a handful who would like to continue with this outdated dinosaur. But what about other citizens? This is supposed to be a democracy, which means that the wishes of the majority should be paramount.

I am sure that dairy farmers don't like it, and mothers with young babies hate it.

Write a few questions down. Think critically about what this writer is saying. Underline any groups of words that you think can be criticised or challenged.

Did you underline 'handful', 'outdated dinosaur', 'ridiculous', 'sigh of relief', 'vast majority', and 'bitter experience' as being exaggerated and biased? How about 'dairy farmers don't like it', 'mothers hate it', and 'vast majority' as being phrases that lack any evidence to support them? And how about 'many problems'? Where are the examples to support this generalisation?

Critical thinkers have words like **consequences, assumptions, accuracy, main point** and **meaning, prejudice, evidence**, as well as **examples, relevance** and **reliability** running through their minds as they judge information they read and hear. If you look at the first letters of these groups of words you come up with the acronym CAMPER!

APPLYING CAMPER

CAMPER is an easy to remember word to remind you of some very probing questions to fire at someone writing or saying some extreme comments about an issue. Try the following questions on someone debating at your next gathering!

C	What are the **consequences** of your actions/belief? How **consistent** is this information...?
A	What **assumptions** are you making here? How **accurate** is this data, statement...?
M	What do you **mean** by...? What is your **main point** here?
P	Why are you so **prejudiced**? What is the other **point of view** here?
E	Where is the **evidence** to support this? Give me an **example** of this.
R	What is the **relevance** of this data, criteria...? How **reliable** is your source, writer, information...?

Here are a few more probing questions for challenging and judging something you read or hear about an issue.

For Seeking Clarification

- What is your main point?
- What do you mean by...?
- Could you give me an example of...?
- Why do you say that?
- Could you explain that further?

For Probing Assumptions Made by Someone

- Aren't you assuming...?
- Why do you think your assumptions hold here?
- Why can't you conclude that...?

For Probing Reasons and Evidence

- What are your reasons for saying that?
- Could you explain your reasons further?
- How do you know that?
- How does that apply here?
- Why did you say that?
- Are these reasons adequate?

For Probing Other Points of View

- What would someone who disagrees with this say?
- Can anyone see this another way?
- Why have you approached this issue from this perspective?
- Have you considered the opposite point of view?
- What are some other points of view?

For Probing Implications and Consequences

- What are you implying by saying that?
- When you say..., are you implying that...?
- What effect will that have?
- If this is the case what else must follow?

For Probing a Question

- Why is this question important?
- Can you restate the question?
- What does this question assume?
- Can you break this question down at all?

SOME CORE CRITICAL THINKING PROCESSES

Fact or Opinion?

Research over the years shows that many people find it difficult to distinguish between statements of facts and statements of opinions. And yet, the Internet, social media, newspapers and magazines contain a mix of these statements every day.

If you want to think critically about what you are reading you need to be able to separate fact from opinion. Check your ability to make such a distinction with the simple task next. After you have done it, reflect on the self-questions or cues that you unconsciously used.

Activity

Which of the four sentences is the only fact? Why aren't the other statements fact?

"Some computers and robots of the next century would be no larger than molecules."

Dr Petty made this comment in a recent issue of the journal, *Signal*.

He felt that the science of nanotechnology was the most challenging in the world today.

"It should produce robots capable of cleaning the walls of our arteries."

Facts are things that you can definitely prove are happening, or have happened in the past. There is evidence to support them. They usually contain definite words such as 'is', 'was', and 'has', or some verb in the past or present tense. They also contain specific information, such as measurements and are statements made by qualified authorities whose reputations are at stake.

Did you mark the second statement, 'Dr Petty made this comment in the recent issue of the journal, *Signal*', as being the fact?

On the other hand, opinions contain indefinite words such as 'could', 'possibly', 'might', and 'should', or words about a person's feelings such as 'suggested', and words about the future such as 'predict'. It is difficult to find evidence to support opinions.

A good critical thinker, when doing this task, might subconsciously ask him or herself questions such as:

▶ *Does this sentence contain words such as 'could', 'may' 'might', 'possibly', 'predict', and 'should'? (opinion)*

▶ *Could this statement be proven experimentally or with evidence? (fact)*

▶ *Is this statement by a reputable authority? (fact)*

▶ *Have the things in this statement actually happened or are they happening now? (fact)*

▶ *Does this statement relate to the feelings of someone (opinion).*

DEFINITE OR INDEFINITE CONCLUSION?

Are you one of those people who jump to conclusions, who make plenty of assumptions, who read between the lines, or who draw inferences or tentative conclusions without any real evidence?

Some people make inferences that are based on assumptions. Critical thinkers, however, are more aware that they are just that – assumptions – and they remind themselves of this when they draw a conclusion.

What can and can't you conclude when you observe a situation first-hand, or when you view some media representation of it?

How did you go?

Here is the bad news. There is no evidence that the boy is the man's son or that the woman is the man's wife. You would be making assumptions about relationships if you concluded these things. There is also no evidence that the man played football. He may even be crying with joy – it is difficult to make definite conclusions about how people feel inside!

It is also difficult to conclude what has happened before this picture, or what is likely to happen after it.

Well, what can you be sure of? There are three people in the picture, the man is sitting down, the boy has a stick, the woman is behind the chair, and there are pictures on the wall. These are all directly observable things. No assumptions are being made.

Definite conclusions involve direct observations. Indefinite conclusions involve assumptions about feelings, things that happened in the past or that might happen in the future, relationships, and so on. You have to be careful when you draw conclusions about the meaning of an advertisement. What can't you be sure of in the advertisement below? What are the 'rubbery' or indefinite words? What can you only make inferences about?

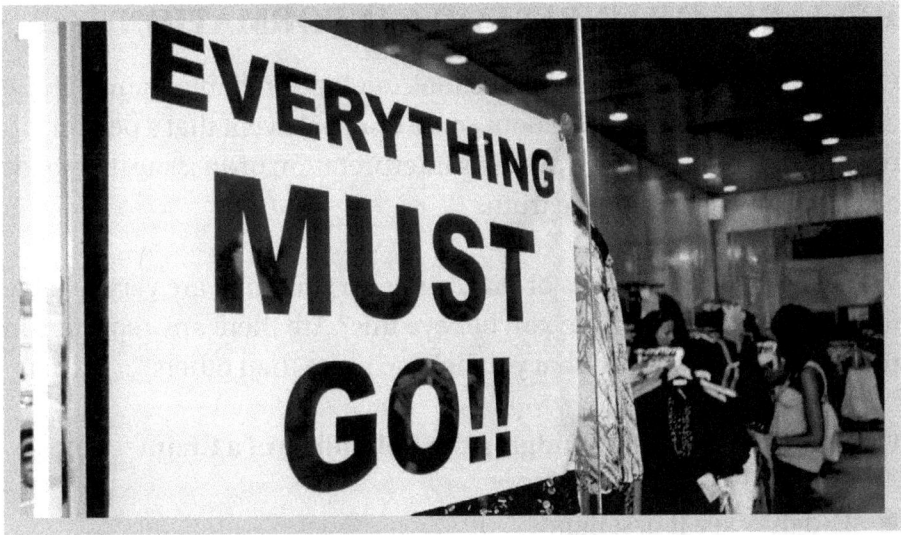

'Everything' is a rubbery word. Does 'everything' mean all things in the store? Or does it mean only storm damaged items, out of fashion garments, or lines that haven't sold? What does 'half price' really mean? Half of the regular price doubled?

Advertising agents are skilled at trying to use words and images that make people jump to conclusions. You might try collecting some clever advertisements and then circling the rubbery words. Make up some funny interpretations as to what the advertisements could mean.

Here are some questions critical thinkers ask themselves when drawing a conclusion after looking at an advertisement, cartoon or picture.

▶ *What are things that can directly observe in this picture or scene? (definite conclusion)*

▶ *Which words here can have a variety of interpretations? (indefinite conclusion)*

▶ *What are some other explanations for this observation? (assumptions that are often made)*

RELIABLE OR UNRELIABLE INFORMATION

Critical thinkers are always on the look out for unreliable claims. These are generally claims made about some unusual event that a person has observed. It may also be a person's interpretation of an issue that reads as though it is a fact, or the truth.

What kinds of newspapers or magazines do you think are very reliable in their reporting? Why do you believe this? Are there any reporters in the newspaper you read that you believe more than others?

Questions to Ask When Judging the Reliability of a Claim

▶ Did they see it first hand?

▶ Did anyone else see it?

▶ Do they have any vested interests in this?

▶ How close were they to the scene?

▶ Were they of sound mind at the time?

▶ Are they well respected by colleagues?

▶ Have they sought publicity about this issue before?

▶ How experienced are they?

▶ Did they report the sighting immediately?

▶ What were the viewing conditions like at the time?

RELEVANT OR IRRELEVANT INFORMATION

What is meant by the relevance of information?

Before you can judge whether something is relevant or irrelevant you first have to be clear about the objective or goal you, or someone else, have in mind. If the information helps you to directly achieve the goal more effectively, then it is relevant.

For example, if your objective is to make a decision on the best choice between two alternatives, then you will want to identify some relevant properties of both things. Here is a decision-making strategy that should help you to make better decisions in the future. At least it will help you to generate some relevant criteria to compare the choices and to then rate or rank each choice against each criterion. The process is still subjective, but at least it forces you to draw a big picture of the overall decision and the choices.

Here are a number of activities to try.

Activity

Imagine you have lost your bicycle. Circle the two most important or RELEVANT things here about your bicycle that you should mention in a LOST BICYCLE notice to place in the newspaper.

a. The cost of the bike.

b. The brand/colour of the bike.

c. The shop were you bought the bike.

d. The month you bought the bike.

e. Where you lost the bike.

f. The speed of the bike.

g. Why you lost the bike.

Possible answers for this activity are the features of the bike ... b and e.

Activity

Imagine that you are about to be ship wrecked on a large island with trees and a mountain. You only have minutes to get off your ship before it sinks. You can only take 4 things from the list below. Which 4 things do you think are the most RELEVANT to take? Number them in order of importance and then give you reasons.

___ Matches   ___ Fresh water

___ Knife   ___ Bed

___ Radio   ___ Plastic sheet

___ Torch   ___ Fishing line

___ Tent   ___ Books

___ Gun   ___ Shovel

Possible answers for this activity are:

◆ Matches for warmth and light
◆ Fresh water to drink and survive
◆ Fishing line for food
◆ Plastic sheet for shelter and to make fresh water via condensation.

Activity

A Decision-Making Strategy

1. You have just won a holiday on a quiz show and have to choose 1 of 4 countries to visit. Which one will you choose? Clearly state the issue or problem.

2. The choices are India, the USA, Italy or Fiji.

3. Now list one or more advantage and disadvantage of each choice.

Country	Advantages	Disadvantages
India	History, cheap	Lack of hygiene
USA	Natural beauty, English spoken	City crimes, expensive
Italy	History, good design, climate	Language, expensive
Fiji	Restful, climate	Limited things to see, history

4. Look over these to select 4 or so relevant criteria with which to compare all choices. State these criteria as a maximum or minimum, e.g. maximum hygiene, maximum beaches, minimum tourists, minimum cost.

5. Rate each choice on a scale or rank each using the comparing criteria. Here are some suggested rankings. The best choice is ranked 1, the worst choice is ranked 4.

Criteria	India	USA	Italy	Fiji
Max. hygiene	4	1	1	3
Max. history	2	3	1	4
Max. climate	4	2	3	1
Max. language	3	1	4	2
Ranking Points	13	7	9	10

6. Select the best choice. The lower the total ranking points the better the choice.

Here, the best choice is the USA. However, you may decide to 'weight' a criterion because it is more important than the others. You can do this by multiplying the ranking points for that criterion by two or three and thus, your total rankings might change.

Decision-making is all about selecting relevant criteria to help you make the best choice between two or more alternatives.

JUDGING BIAS

Bias can be thought of as favouring or not favouring a particular item or group of people.

This may be in a written or picture statement. In judging bias critical thinkers often have self-questions such as those listed below.

Questions to Ask When Judging Bias

▶ Is this group only in a helping rather than a leading role?

▶ Is this group mainly shown as being frightened or lazy?

▶ ls this group only in dependent, non-professional roles?

▶ Is this group mainly shown in the background?

▶ Is this group only shown in safe, passive activities?

There are plenty of examples of cartoons, pictures, and pieces of writing on the Internet, social media, in newspapers and magazines that provide good example of biased reporting.

Distinguishing facts from opinions, definite from indefinite conclusions, relevant from less relevant factors, biased from non-biased language, and reliable from unreliable information are only a few of the critical thinking processes we use regularly.

KEY POINTS

☑ Critical thinking involves making judgements of information with the use of relevant criteria.

☑ Strong critical thinkers are COOL. They clarify, are objective, are open-minded, and are loose or flexible.

☑ Critical thinkers ask themselves questions about CAMPER: consequences, assumptions, meaning/main points, prejudice, evidence/examples and relevance/reliability.

CHAPTER 9

WHAT IS YOUR THINKING STYLE?

Pre-reading questions to ponder:

- ◆ Why do the thinking styles of people differ?
- ◆ Is your thinking style fixed for life?
- ◆ Are there advantages of thinking in a particular way?
- ◆ How many styles of thinking are there?

THINKING STYLES AND INTELLIGENCES

Many different cognitive styles, learning styles, and what I will call thinking styles, have been identified by different researchers. Many of these are influenced by our personality and temperament, as we will see in this chapter.

Our thinking style, once formed, is also very strongly related to the strength of our various intelligences. For example, very focused and analytical people will probably have a strong mathematical-logical intelligence. On the other hand, those with a non-focused, 'big picture' style will probably have a strong visual-spatial intelligence. They could also have a strong interpersonal intelligence due to their sensitivity to the whole field of information that comes in their interactions with others.

You might be asking, 'What determines our personality and temperament?' I suggest that our body chemistry and earlier life experiences play a big part here. Personality influences whether we are more internally or externally motivated and whether we see the world in a more focused or non-focused way. It also influences whether we like things finished rather than left open-ended and whether we are more objective and logical than subjective and emotional.

A variety of dimensions have been suggested for the development of our personality. These mix to give us a particular personality type and hence a particular thinking style. We all have a little of the extremes of each of the following dimensions. In other words, we each fit somewhere along the ruler for each dimension.

One of the most researched 'single dimension' cognitive style is that of field independence and field dependence. Some people are very focused and relatively unaffected by the field of information surrounding the thing they are focusing on. We say they are field independent. On the other hand, field dependents tend to be non-focused, sociable, interactive and like to receive feedback. People will respond to an activity like this differently.

Activity

How many triangles are there in this figure?

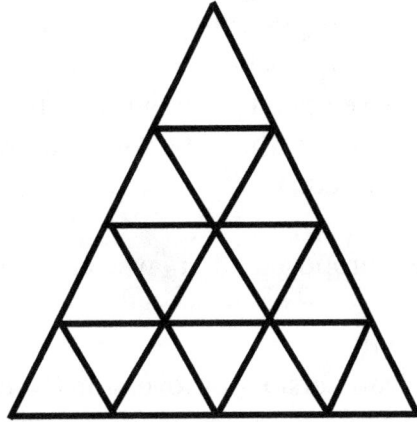

The answer for the activity is 27! The fewer you answer the more field dependent you are.

Here are some personality characteristics that have been associated with people who are more field dependent or field independent. They will certainly affect the way you think about issues and problems.

Field Dependent	Field Independent
Non-focused	Focused
Co-operative	Competitive
Interactive	Independent
Likes feedback	Doesn't need feedback
Social	Impersonal
Global	Analytical
Needs external goals	Sets own goals
Likes group projects	Likes independent projects

MYERS BRIGGS AND TEMPERAMENT TEST

The learning or thinking style I want to particularly focus on here is the one which has been researched and applied more than any other. It was developed by Isabel Myers Briggs and is based on the psychology of Carl Jung. This time four dimensions, rather than one or two, are intertwined.

Jung proposed that we each have four main dimensions of temperament:

1. Extroversion–Introversion (E versus I).

2. Sensing–Intuition (S versus N).

3. Thinking–Feeling (T versus F).

4. Perceiving/Open–Judging/Closure (P versus J).

The following tables describe each of these dimensions. There are 16 combinations of these four variables called temperament types. Now let's see which of these temperament types you have.

E	I
I'm happiest when I am with a large group of people. I like to start talking to people, even strangers. I'm fairly easy to approach. I do my fair share of talking in conversations.	I'm happiest when I am with only one or two people. I usually wait until people start talking to me. I'm more reserved and difficult to approach. I tend to do more listening in conversations.

N	S
I'm interested in fantasies or possibilities. I like to do things in novel and different ways. I'm more interested in things in the future. I tend to miss fine details in things I look at. I am fairly imaginative and speculative, and often go on hunches.	I'm more interested in facts or real experiences. I like to do things in proven ways that work. I'm more interested in current or past things. I notice fine details in things that I look at. I am fairly realistic, sensible, and practical.

F	T
I'm a fairly logical person. I tend to hide my feelings. I make choices based on logical criteria. I'm embarrassed when other people show their emotions. Objective, analysis, policy, standards are words that I relate to.	I'm a sentimental person. I usually show my feelings. I tend to make choices based on my feelings. I don't mind when other people show their emotions. Subjective, values, personal harmony, devotion are words that I relate to.

J	P
I like to have things finished I like deadlines. I'm more decisive. I like to plan ahead. Settled, completed, planned, fixed, deadlines are words that I relate to.	I like things unfinished. I hate deadlines. I'm more indecisive. I tend to let things happen. Tentative, open-ended, flexible are words that I relate to.

Now write down the four letters that you have circled at the top of the four columns that best describe you. This is your temperament type.

My temperament type is: ___ ___ ___ ___

Amongst the four letters of your temperament type there will be the letters:

SJ or **SP** or **NF** or **NT**

Circle the pair of letters that is in your temperament type.

This is now called your temperament. As you can see there are four main temperaments.

My temperament is: ___ ___

Researchers have linked these temperaments to different styles of learning, teaching, managing, and mateship.

THINKING STYLE AND TEMPERAMENT

Learning styles are of interest here because they relate to thinking styles. Here is a summary of the four learning styles that are linked with the four temperaments. The percentages quoted in the tables here are based on studies done during the 1980s to 1990s period, and still hold some relevance today.

SJ style

Rely on real experience and like things finished

No wonder 36% of people and 56% of teachers have this style.

SJs like goals, structure, feedback, routines, lectures, subjects about the lives of people as found in history, geography, business and social studies.

They are secure with the norm and authority and hence make traditional leaders. They are also faithful and reliable friends.

SP style

Rely on real experience and leave things open

SPs represent 38% of the population and 2% of teachers.

They are 'hands on' people who like group work, competition and risk-taking. They are verbal/visual learners who often reject rules and authority. They like jumping from one thing to the next. SPs like music, drama, art, craft and mechanics.

SPs are troubleshooters and good negotiators and make energetic, creative and artistic mates.

NF style

Intuitive feelers

NFs have a gift for languages, talking and vivid imagery.

They are charming, attract others, and like group interaction and feedback. They are idealists and dramatic, and are attracted to people-oriented subjects.

NFs represent 12% of the population and 36% of teachers. They are catalytic leaders who bring out the best in people. They are also very romantic mates.

NT style

Intuitive thinkers

NTs represent 12% of the population and 6% of teachers.

They are often curious, independent, logical thinkers who can be academic snobs and high achievers. They like experimentation, choice and justice! Maths and science are favourites.

NTs are visionary leaders and excellent role models but they can be cold, self-absorbed mates!

It is my belief that our personality or temperament influences the way we think about, and react to, information. Our temperament must also affect our values, our interests, our motivation to attend to particular issues and our willingness to think analytically, critically and creatively.

By considering how we and some of our friends or colleagues answered the temperament test here, we may start to appreciate why we can think and feel quite differently about some common information that is being shared. Thinking styles are different from thinking strategies. Thinking styles colour our thinking.

CHANGING YOUR THINKING STYLE

Our intelligences are changing every day. By now, I hope you accept the fact that we can learn strategies for improving any one of our intelligences. It is far more difficult and long term to change your personality and temperament, if this is even possible at all.

However, if you learn ways of thinking more logically or interpersonally then these should help you to hurry up the process of a 'personality change'!

It is hard to place a value on a style of thinking. Sometimes it is good to think in a focused way and in other circumstances it is better to be non-focused. It is good to be able to be flexible when it comes to thinking styles.

KEY POINTS

☑ We each have different thinking styles that are influenced by our personalities and the strength of our various intelligences.

☑ Our temperament type influences our learning style, and our style as a manager, a teacher and a mate.

☑ Our style of thinking colours the way we think about issues.

CHAPTER 10

IMPROVING YOUR MEMORY

Pre-reading questions to ponder:

- What is the principle behind memory aids?
- What are strategies to help remember things?
- How can music help memory?

I KNOW YOUR FACE

You obviously need to remember content if you want to improve any intelligence. But remembering is not easy. Have you ever wondered why it is much easier to remember someone's face rather than their name, or why it is much easier to remember the tune of a song rather than its actual words?

Pictures (faces) and patterns (tunes) are usually stored in our memories as part of an inter-connected network. These larger networks of information are reasonably easy to retrieve from our memories. On the other hand, words, names, numbers, and similar facts are much harder to recall, because they are not usually linked with a larger pattern or picture. We tend to store such things as isolated or unconnected 'bits' of information.

On this basis, people who are strong in visual-spatial and music-rhythmic intelligence should be really good at remembering things because they are good at creating and storing mental pictures and rhythms. Check this out with yourself and your friends! Are math-logical thinkers good at remembering things?

WHAT ARE MNEMONICS?

Mnemonics are strategies to help us remember information. They rely on the linking of 'pictureless' names to a picture or pattern that we create. Such pictures and patterns act as memory aids.

Mnemonics include:

- ◆ Acronyms
- ◆ Acrostics
- ◆ Paired associates
- ◆ Points on a path.

ACRONYMS

Imagine that you have to remember the four stages in the life-cycle of a fly; namely the adult, pupa, egg, and larva stages.

Questions to Ask Yourself:

▶ What are the first letters of the words to remember?

▶ Can I rearrange these letters to form a single word?

If you can form a single word, such as 'pale' or 'peal' in this case, it is known as an acronym. The idea is that it is much easier to remember a single word, or a meaningful pattern of letters, than a series of words. Once the acronym has been learnt, each letter acts as a reminder of which letters the separate words you had to remember begin with.

ACROSTICS

Imagine that you had to remember the names of the first six planets, in order of their respective distance from the Sun. They are Mercury, Venus, Earth, Mars, Jupiter, Saturn.

Questions to Ask Yourself:

▶ What are the first letters of the words to remember?

▶ Can I rearrange these letters to form a single word? No!

▶ Can I form a funny sentence, with each word starting with the first letters of the words I have to remember?

The funny sentence is called an acrostic. It is a pattern of meaningful and hopefully funny words. For example, the letters of the names to remember are M V E M J S.

Many sentences are possible. My sentence is:

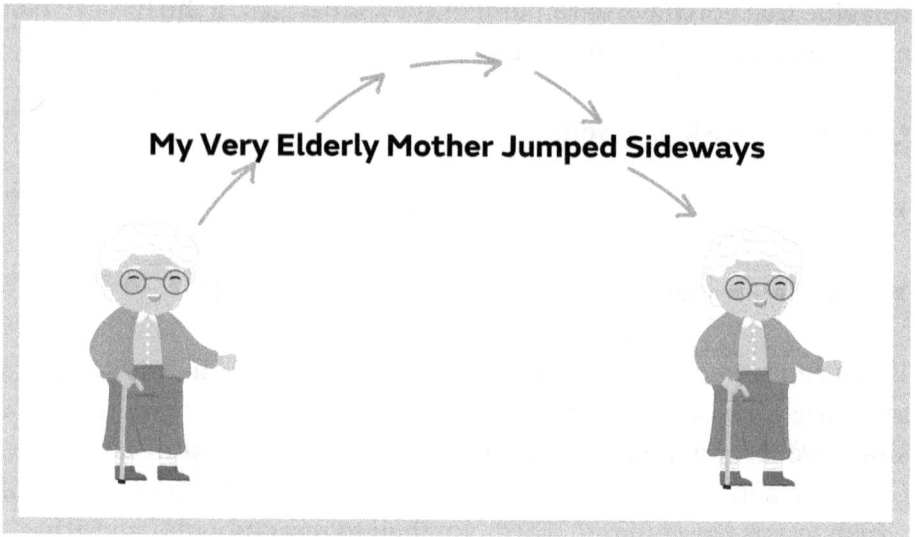

My Very Elderly Mother Jumped Sideways

Notice how the first letters of these words give me a reminder as to the first letters of the names to remember.

You may have quite a different sentence but the words in it must start with the first letters of the words to remember.

Music teachers have always been particularly fond of acrostics.

Every Good Boy Deserves Fruit

Is the most common way of remembering the names of the lines on the treble clef stave (EGBDF).

E G B D F

PAIRED ASSOCIATES

In this strategy the idea is to pair a name or thing to remember with a funny or extreme picture. For example, if you have to remember a person's name as Mr Rose, picture his face with a giant rose stuck on top of his head or his face with a pair of rose earrings. Next time you see his face, the funny image you have associated with his name will come back to you. Oh! he is the person with the giant rose on top. Hello Mr Rose.

When learning a foreign language there are many words to remember. For example, the word for 'map' in Spanish is 'carta'. So pair the word 'map' by placing a huge map in a supermarket cart. Now you will easily recall that 'map' and 'cart' (or carta) go together.

POINTS ON A PATH

The first thing you need here is a picture in your mind of some points on a path or route that is really familiar to you. It may be the houses in your street, the holes on your golf course, the rooms in your house, and so on. Now, you need to place the things that you have to remember at separate points along the path. These should be placed in an extreme or funny way.

Imagine that you had to remember some exports to other countries such as sugar, cars, fish, flowers and rice. In the garden of the first house in your street you might place some giant sugar cubes, in the garden of the next house a pile of smashed up cars, in the next a large snapper across the driveway, in the next flowers growing all over the roof and, in the next, bags of rice coming out of the chimney. The brain has a wonderful memory for such extreme or funny pictures. Once you recall the houses in your street, the things associated with them also come back.

Use one of the strategies discussed here to remember the following lists of things. Choose wisely and then get a friend to check your memory. Allow five minutes between learning your list and the testing of it. Remember:

- Acronyms are used to remember words.
- Acrostics are used when you want to remember words in a fixed sequence.
- Paired associates are used to remember more visual objects.
- Points on a path are used when you want to remember visual objects in a sequence.

Activity

Use an appropriate mnemonic to remember the names in each of the following groups.

1. These parts of the eye: iris, pupil, retina, eyeball, lens.

2. These European countries: France, Germany, Spain, Italy.

3. These English kings in this order: Edward, George, Charles, James.

4. These products in this order: carrots, beer, chairs, lights, letters.

Possible Answers are:

1. An acronym, PLIER: P for pupil, L for lens, I for iris, E for eyeball, and R for retina.

2. An acronym, FIGS: F for France, I for Italy, G for Germany, and S for Spain.

3. An acrostic: Every Good Child Jumps!

4. Points on a path: Imagine coming home to find a huge carrot stretched across your driveway, beer cans nailed to your front door, a stack of chairs in your hallway, Christmas lights flashing in your bedroom, and piles and piles of letters in the toilet next door.

SUGGESTOPAEDIA

If you found that these mnemonics didn't help much there is still hope. You can encourage your brain to produce its own memory-enhancing chemicals that help you remember things. These chemicals include beta endorphins and enkephalins. The secret is to relax your brain! You can do this by playing background music at 72 beats per minute, the natural pulse rate of the body, while you are trying to remember something.

The science of Suggestopaedia, developed in Bulgaria during the late 1960s, is used to study such a phenomenon. It has been used by foreign language departments in universities to help students remember vocabulary more effectively. Students who have the advantage of Baroque music playing in the background show greater accuracy of recall.

Baroque music is helping other kinds of learning other than memorising.

For example, a university in America reported that students listening to Baroque music, learnt a spatial reasoning task involving paper folding, much better than students who didn't have the advantage of the music.

Baroque music can certainly increase the concentration of memory-enhancing chemicals in the brain. However, it also activates the right hemisphere of the brain while the left brain is busy trying to remember foreign language words or any other terms, names, and similar isolated 'bits' of information. Both halves of the brain become active.

Without the help of music there would be little right brain activity when learning word lists unless the student was trying to visualise images associated with each word. The right brain remembers patterns, rhythms, and pictures extremely efficiently. With the right brain activated by the music the more abstract, 'pictureless' foreign language vocabulary is somehow more easily associated with the rhythms of the music.

DEEP PROCESSING

Deep processing is another strategy for remembering a recorded or real life experience. It relies on you using as many senses as you can.

The idea is to:

- Shut your eyes and try to create a clear, still or moving mental picture of the situation or event.
- Talk to yourself about the person, place, or things you see in your picture.
- Try to focus on some vivid smell, taste, or feeling that you think is associated with your mental picture.
- Try to focus on a particular emotion such as sadness, happiness, anger, or excitement that you associate with your picture.

Deep processing relies on you making many and varied 'connections' between the images, sensations, and feelings related to an experience. The greater the number of connections, the greater the possibility of recalling the experience as you have built a large network of related information in your memory. It has been known for many years that young children who are encouraged to 'deep process' after reading a story, show a much greater ability to recall and understand the information in the story.

Remembering information is supposed to be the simplest kind of thinking, because you don't have to ask yourself any questions about the information you are trying to remember. You are simply trying to 'plug' some bits of information in your memory. However, it is often difficult to recall these bits, because they haven't been connected to other related information. Nonetheless, by using the mnemonics suggested in this chapter you can significantly improve your ability to download the content of your own super computer-your brain.

KEY POINTS

☑ It is easier to remember words if you can link them to pictures or rhymes, especially funny ones!

☑ Relax the brain if you want it to produce its own memory enhancing chemicals.

☑ Certain types of music can help improve your memory.

APPENDIX A

ANSWERS FOR PROBING CREATIVE DESIGNS

POSSIBLE ANSWERS

1. **Most coins are round.**

   Easy to make
   Easy to stack/store
   Easy to put in slots
   So you don't cut hands/clothing

2. **Most animals have 4 legs and not 2 like humans.**

   Can run faster
   Don't need hands to feed self
   Can run on 3 legs if broken
   Can kick to defend self
   Can jump higher

3. **Bees have wings.**

   To fly up to flowers
   To escape enemies
   To carry nectar to hives
   To cover large distances looking for nectar in flowers

4. **Fish have scales.**

   Can swim faster
   To protect soft flesh
   Can escape human hands

5. **Pencils are made of wood.**

   Easy to sharpen
   Soft to hold
   Easy to store

6. **Jars are made of glass.**

   Easy to see what is inside
   Easy to wash
   Easy to recycle
   Easy to melt into shape

7. **Australian footballs are oval in shape and not round.**

   Easier to catch
   Easier to kick accurately/long distances
   Easier to hand ball
   Unpredictable bounces

8. **Flowers are coloured.**

   Attract bees
   People pick to prune and encourage new growth
   Show different types of flowers

9. **Elephants have large ears.**

   To cool blood in their veins
   To swat flies near mouth
   To match size of their bodies

10. **Chairs have 4 legs and not 6.**

    Better balance on 4
    Less cluttered look
    Easier to fix to seat
    Cheaper to make

11. **Insects are usually very small.**

    Can hide in small places
    Parent can lay hundreds of eggs
    Insects

12. Giraffes have very long necks

To see approaching enemies a long way away
To reach leaves they like to eat at top of trees
To keep brain a long way away from animals attacking their body

13. Newspapers have very large pages compared to the pages of a book

Easy to roll up for throwing
Easy to pulp and recycle
Easy to print in machines
Cover many topics on a page
Easy to read sitting down
Easy to stack in piles

APPENDIX B

THE LANGREHR TEST OF CREATIVE THINKING

Aim: to test the cautious judgment of information using relevant criteria.

Items used: ability to identify facts/opinions, relevant/irrelevant factors, sure/unsure conclusions, reliable/unreliable claims, different points of view.

Time limit: about 30 to 40 minutes

Answer acceptance: if necessary each answer must be agreed as being realistic by a majority taking the test.

For thinkers who can write responses.

NAME: _____

One mark for each possible answer.

1. List 4 things that you **could not SEE.**

   1.
   2.
   3.
   4.

   4 points

2. List 3 reasons why fish have scales.

   1.
   2.
   3.

   3 points

3. List 3 places where you could not read a newspaper.

   1.
   2.
   3.

   3 points

4. List 4 quite different uses for some string other than to tie things up.

    1.
    2.
    3.
    4.

4 points

5. List 3 ways of getting a TABLE TENNIS ball out of a glass jar without touching the glass or the ball with your hands.

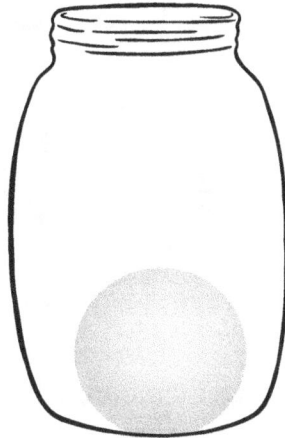

    1.
    2.
    3.

3 points

6. List 6 quite different things the line drawing here could represent.

1.
2.
3.
4.
5.
6.

6 x ½ = 3 points

7. What if there was no longer a moon. What are 3 things that would happen?

1.
2.
3.

3 points

POSSIBLE ANSWERS

1. **List 4 things that you could not SEE.**

   Infinity
   An idea
   A dream
   The universe
   Live dinosaur
   Person long dead
   Centre of Earth

   4 points

2. **List 3 reasons why fish have scales.**

   To slip from human hands
   To protect flesh from bites or sharp surfaces
   To glide quicker through water
   To keep warm

   3 points

3. **List 3 places where you couldn't read a newspaper.**

   Under water
   In the dark without a light
   If paper in foreign language
   While parachuting from plane

   3 points

4. **List 4 quite different uses for some string other than to tie things up.**

Shoe laces
Clothes line
Fishing line
Tie up hands
Spin a top
Pull a toy car
Lead for dog,

4 points

5. **List 3 ways of getting a TABLE TENNIS ball out of a glass jar without touching the ball or the glass.**

Pour liquid in to overflow
Suck up with straw or vacuum cleaner
Stick tape on end of a straw and lift
Stick with pin or nail stuck in end to prick and lift

3 points

6. **List 6 quite different things the line drawing here could represent.**

Mountains
Broken glass
Birds mouths
Graph
Stalactites
Road
Hat
Flames
Teeth

Lightning
Waves
Tents

6 x ½ = 3 points

7. **What if there was no longer a moon. What are 3 things that would happen?**

Very dark at night
No tides
Less fish caught
More electricity used in world
No rockets fired at moon
Less money spent on space explorations

3 points

Total = 23 points

APPENDIX C

THE LANGREHR TEST OF CRITICAL THINKING

Aim: to test imagination, flexibility of thought, open mindedness.

Items used: ability to suggest unusual uses, things represented by a diagram, and imaginative consequences, comparisons, combinations, reversals, solutions, alternatives.

Time limit: about 30 minutes (creativity can't be forced).

Answer acceptance: if necessary each answer must be agreed as being realistic by a majority taking the test.

For thinkers who can write responses.

NAME: _____

One mark for each possible answer.

1. Write down 3 things to tell people that would **HELP** them to find your LOST DOG

3 points

Write down 3 things to tell people that would **NOT HELP** them to find your LOST DOG.

3 points

2. Write down 3 things that would **HELP** you believe a friend who claims to have seen a flying saucer hover over his house last night.

3 points

Write down 3 things that would **NOT HELP** you to believe a friend who claims to have seen a flying saucer hover over his house last night.

3 points

3. Write down 3 **FACTS** you know about dogs.

3 points

Write down 3 things that are only **OPINIONS** about dogs. You can't prove them.

3 points

4. Write down 3 things in **FAVOR** of using windmills to make electricity.

3 points

Write down 3 things **AGAINST** using windmills to make electricity.

3 points

5. Mr Reader didn't receive his morning newspaper in the driveway as usual. He assumed the paper delivery man must be sick. What is he assuming? Name 3 other things that could be the reason for no newspaper being in his driveway?

3 points

6. Your boat is shipwrecked on a distant island. What will you take to survive for maybe a few days or a week? Write down 3 things that you think **ARE IMPORTANT** to take to the island from your wreck.

3 points

Write down 3 things that you think **AREN'T VERY IMPORTANT** to take to the island from your wreck.

3 points

Total 33 points

POSSIBLE ANSWERS

1. **List 3 things to tell people that would help them to find your LOST DOG.**

   Breed of dog
   Colour of dog
   Size of dog

   3 points

   List 3 things to tell people that would not help them to find your LOST DOG.

   When lost
   Cost of dog
   Where dog sleeps
   Sex of dog
   What dog eats

   3 points

2. **List 3 things that would help you to believe a friend who claims to have seen a flying saucer hover over his house.**

   He used telescope
   Took a photo
   Others saw it
   Saw it for 10 minutes

   3 points

List 3 things to tell people that would not help them to find your LOST DOG.

He was not of sound body or mind
He often reported seeing UFOs
No one else saw the UFO
No picture was taken

3 points

3. **Write down 3 things that you think are facts about dogs.**

4 legs
Can bark
Can't climb trees
Can be a pet
Can learn tricks

3 points

Three things that are only opinions about dogs. You can't prove them.

Smarter than cats
Better pets than cats
Have annoying bark
Should sleep outside

3 points

4. **Write down 3 things for using windmills to make electricity.**

Don't give off gases
Cheap electricity
Few people needed to work equipment
No factory needed
No coal or oil used up

3 points

Write down 3 things against using windmills to make electricity.

Noisy on farms
Need wind to work
Look ugly on farmland
Costly to set up

3 points

5. **Three other reasons Mr Reader didn't get any morning newspaper in his driveway.**

Someone stole it
Delivery man had an accident
Newspaper was not printed today
The delivery threw it next door by accident
The paper went under a bush

3 points

6. **List 3 things that you think are important to take to the island from your wreck.**

Water to drink
Matches for warmth
Sail or blanket to shelter under
Mirror to signal
Fishing line to catch fish to eat

3 points

List 3 things that you think are not very important to take to the island.

A book
A radio,
A TV
A map
Oars

3 points

Total = 33 points

APPENDIX D

THE LANGREHR TEST OF EARLY CHILDHOOD THINKING

The Langrehr Test of Early Childhood Thinking (LTECT) tests the ability of children age 5 to 8 to think for themselves. It is not a test of simple memory.

The first 4 items of the test assess different thinking processes or skills associated with creative thinking. The items assess creative flexibility. The last 4 items assess different thinking processes or skills associated with critical or judgmental thinking.

PRESENTING THE TEST

This is an **oral test** and is to be given to only one child at a time.

Carefully read the question at the top of each sheet to the child. If he/she is not sure of what the question means then clarify it in your words. Clarify, **but do not give hints or other examples** to help the child answer the question.

Maximum time is 1 minute per question. Most children will give up before this time so tell them to say 'finish' when they can't come up with any more answers for a question. Don't rush them.

RECORDING ANSWERS

A range of acceptable answers can be given for each item. A student only receives one mark for each acceptable category suggested. A student may give more than one example from the same category; however, only one of these examples scores a mark for the category. Other acceptable categories may be accepted within a school. As long as the marking is consistent this will not effect the marking or selection of students within a school.

QUESTION 1

Here is a funny drawing.
What does it remind you of?
What else could it be? (child's response).
What else could it be? (repeat until no more answers).

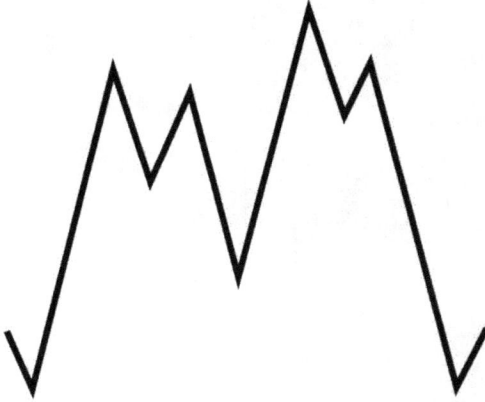

QUESTION 2

Here is a newspaper that people read.
I wonder what **other things** you can use a newspaper for?
Can you tell me some?

QUESTION 3

What are some ways in which a door and a book are the SAME?

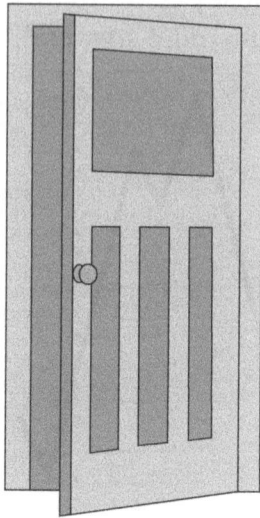

QUESTION 4

You can see most things with your eyes. But I know some things that **you can't see**. Can you tell me some?

QUESTION 5

Here is a picture of a cute puppy dog.
When you look at the picture are you really sure that
1) the puppy has its tongue hanging down? Yes or no?
2) the puppy is thirsty? Yes or no?
3) the puppy has been on a long run? Yes or no?

QUESTION 6

Think of some cats and dogs that you have seen. Would everyone think, (or be able to prove) that:

 ◆ Cats can climb trees better than dogs?
 ◆ Cats are prettier than dogs?
 ◆ Dogs make better pets than cats?

QUESTION 7

Would it help you to find this lost dog if you knew
1. How much the owner paid for the dog? Yes or no?
2. The colour and type of dog it is? Yes or no?
3. When the owner bought the dog? Yes or no?

QUESTION 8

Let's pretend that there were **no more trees in the world**? What are some things that animals and people **would not have any more**?

SUGGESTED ANSWERS AND SCORING

1. **One mark for each of the suggested categories below.**

birds/fish	mouths	crack	crown
flames	fingers	glass broken	graph
hair	icicles	lightning	mountains
pyramids	scribble	stalactites	teeth
tents	waves	2 Ms	

   4 points

   Testing visual creativity and imagination

2. **Maximum mark is 3 for any 3 of the categories below. More than 1 example from the same category does not score extra marks.**

   Flammable – light fires
   Cleaner – tables, walls, books, windows
   Cover – tables, walls, books, windows
   Packing – glasses
   Crafts – make kite, hat, paper mache
   Absorber of liquids

   3 points

   Testing creative uses

3. **Maximum mark is 3 for an example from 3 of the categories below. More than 1 example from the same category does not score extra marks.**

Same shape – rectangular
Man made – not alive
Made from tree/wood
Can open both
Found in homes
Have a front/back/sides

3 points

Testing creative similarities

4. **Maximum mark is 3 for an example from 3 of the categories below. More than 1 example from the same category does not score extra marks.**

Mental processes – ideas, emotions, feelings, memories, thoughts
Things long dead – dinosaurs, people lond dead
Concepts – heaven, hall, time, evil, songs, sounds
Spiritual – god, devil, angels
Gases – space, air/gassess

3 points

Testing creative reversals

5. **One mark for each yes/no question.**

    In this picture are you sure that:
    1. The dog has its tounge hanging down. Yes or no? **Answer Yes**
    2. The dog is thirsty? Yes or no? **Answer No.**
    3. The dog has been on a long run? Yes or no? **Answer No.**

    3 points

    Testing distriguishing sure from unsure conclusions

6. **One mark for each yes/no question.**

    Would everyone tink that
    1. Cats climb trees better than dogs? Yes or no? **Answer Yes**
    2. Cats are prettier than dogs? Yes or no? **Answer No.**
    3. Dogs make better pets than cats? Yes or no? **Answer No.**

    3 points

    Testing distriguishing facts from opinions.

7. **One mark for each yes/no question.**

    1. How much owner paid for dog? Yes or no? **Answer No**
    2. The colour and the type? Yes or no? **Answer Yes.**
    3. When the owner bought the dog? Yes or no? **Answer No.**

    3 points

    Testing distriguishing relevant from less relevant

8. **Maximum mark is 3 for an example from 3 of the categories below. More than 1 example from the same category does not score extra marks.**

Less wood
Less shade
Less places for birds to hide/sleep/rest
Less oxygen for us
Less leaves
Hotter

3 points

Testing ability to identify future consequences.

Total = 25 points

APPENDIX E

DINOSAURS THEMATIC UNIT

Students can learn some good questions for the core thinking processes shown in Chapter 1. Then they have to be able to apply these questions to other topics including those that interest them outside of school. Here is an example of some questions on a dinsoaur theme, that will encourage students to practice some of the core thinking processes.

DINOSAURS

Dinosaurs or 'terrible lizards' weren't lizards at all. Rather, they were cold-blooded reptiles that lived on Earth between 225 and 65 million years ago. Some were plant-eaters while others were flesh-eaters. Some were up to 27 metres long and would have been able to look over a three-storey building, while others were less than a metre long. Also, they could weigh up to 85 tons, or 10 times the weight of an elephant.

The bones and footprints of dead dinosaurs were covered with mud millions of years ago. Under the pressure of layers and layers of soil, this mud turned to hard rock. Today scientists find very old bones, footprints and shells in this rock that help them to picture what life was like millions of years ago. These preserved bones and prints are called fossils.

The dinosaurs lived on the Earth when it was warm and humid. Some dinosaurs, like Tyrannosaurus, did not like the water while others, like Diplodocus, spent most of the day in lakes.

Below is a table of some more properties of five of the dinosaurs.

Dinosaur	Lays Eggs	Sharp Teeth	Neck Length	Meat Eating	Number of Legs	Small Brain
Tyrannosaurus	Yes	Yes	Short	Yes	4	Yes
Diplodocus	Yes	No	Long	No	4	Yes
Stegosaurus	Yes	No	Short	No	4	Yes
Trachodon	YEs	No	Short	No	4	Yes
Triceratops	Yes	No	Short	No	4	Yes

Here are a range of themetic thinking activites that can be used in a classroom. Suggested answers are at the end.

1. Comparing

A Diplodocus and an elephant are the same in some ways but different in others. In the table below, write in 3 things that apply to a Diplodocus only, 3 things that apply to an elephant only, and 3 things that both have in common.

Diplodocus Only	Both	Elephant only

2. Categorising

1 of the following dinosaurs is different from the other 3. Write its name in Group 1. Explain why it is different.

a) Tyrannosaurus
b) Stegosaurus
c) Trachodon
d) Triceratops

Group 1	Reason Why it is Difference

3. Making generalisations

Allosaurus was a dinosaur. List 4 things you can be sure of about Allosaurus even without looking them up.

a)   c)

b)   d)

Megasaurus is a reptile in South America that lays eggs, has 4 legs, eats plants, and has a small brain. Is it a dinosaur? Why or why not?

a)

b)

4. Identifying causes and effects

Underline the cause and circle the effect in the following:

a) The Diplodocus ran into the lake as the Tyrannosaurus came over the hill.

b) The Diplodocus, with its large body and small head, ate quickly most of the day before it came from the lake.

5. Making inferences and seeking evidence

Fred concluded that dinosaurs died out because they ran out of food on the Earth.

What was Fred assuming? In other words, what else could have killed off the dinosaurs?

6. Predicting

a) The dinosaur called Camptosaurus protected itself by running and hiding behind trees. What do you predict about its:

Size?
Food?
Teeth?

b) The dinosaur called Stegosaurus had soft teeth, it couldn't run quickly, it couldn't swim, and it couldn't hide easily. How do you think it protected itself?

c) The dinosaur called Anatosaurus had sharp teeth and webbed feet. What do you think it ate?

7. Creative thinking – reverse thinking

a) List two types of animals that Tyrannosaurus could not catch and eat.

b) The answer is dinosaur. List four questions with this answer.

    1.

    2.

    3.

    4.

8. Creative thinking – consequences

Complete this sentence:

If scientists today created dinosaurs in the laboratory then ...

9. Analytical thinking - designs

a) Why did the Diplodocus need such a long neck?

b) Why did dinosaurs, like other reptiles, lay eggs rather than have live babies?

10. Distinguishing facts from opinions

Which 2 of the following statements are facts?

a) Some day, scientists could breed dinosaurs in the laboratory.

b) Dinosaurs were not warm blooded.

c) Dinosaurs needed oxygen to live.

d) Dinosaurs died out because smaller animals ate their eggs.

Say why you think they are facts!

11. Distinguishing good from poor reasoning

Sue reasons that:

The Diplodocus was one of the largest dinosaurs. Therefore it must have been one of the fiercest and most frightening of the dinosaurs.

Why is this poor reasoning?

What is Sue assuming?

12. Judging reliability

A scientist claims to have found a dinosaur egg out in the desert near his campsite. Write down the 3 most important things for you to know before believing his story.

a)

b)

c)

13. Designing your own questions

Use the question generator to design 3 of your own questions about dinosaurs. Then see if you can find answers for them.

a)

b)

c)

14. Making connections and self-questioning

Write in 1 to 5 words along each arrow in the diagram below to make sensible sentences starting with Dinosaurs and ending with the word in each box.

Ask yourself 'Why?' after each sentence. Try to find the answers, either by yourself, or in groups.

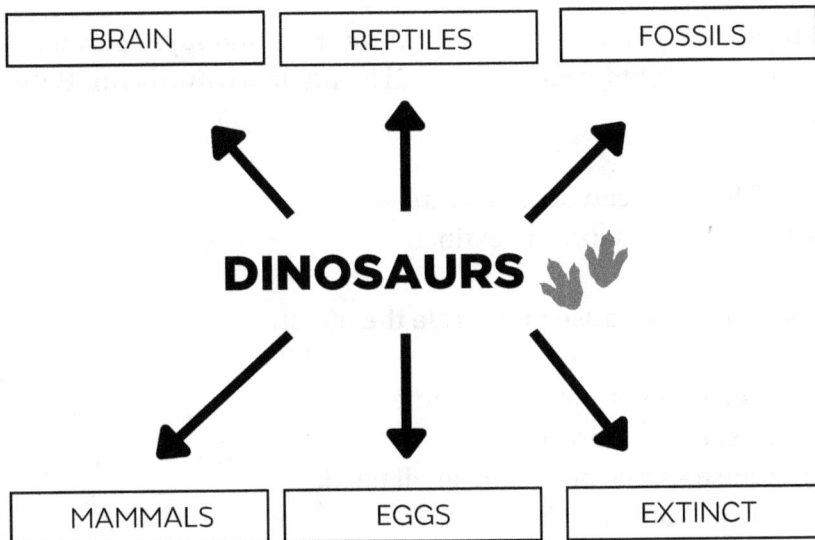

BRAIN	REPTILES	FOSSILS

DINOSAURS

MAMMALS	EGGS	EXTINCT

SOME POTENTIAL ANSWERS

1. Write 3 things that apply to a Diplodocus only, 3 things that apply to an elephant only and 3 things that have both in common.

    Diplodocus only – extinct, reptile, long neck, small head, cold-blooded, egg laying.
    Elephant only – living, mammal, short tail, large head, warm blooded, young born live.
    Both – plant eaters, four big legs, short tail, large body, like water.

2. One of the dinosaurs is different from the others 3. Write its name and say which it is different.

    Tyrannosaurus – meat eater/sharp teeth.

3. Allosaurus was a dinosaur. List 4 things you can be sure of about Allosaurus even without looking them up.

    Laid eggs
    Four legs
    Reptile/cold-blooded
    Small brain

    Megasurus is a reptile in South America that lays eggs, has four legs, eats plants, and has a small brain. It is a dinosaur. Why and why not?

    Why? Reptiles can be dinosaurs.
    Why not? Dinosaurs are extinct.

4. Underline the cause and circle the effect.

    a) Cause – Tyrannosaurus came.
        Effect – ran into lake.
    b) Cause – large body and small head.
        Effect – ate quickly.

5. **What was Fred assuming? In other words, what else could have killed off the dinosaurs?**

   Something ate their eggs, a change in climate, cold killed them, a disease/virus killed them.

6. **a) The dinosaur called Camptosaurus protected itself by running and hiding behind trees. What do you predict about its: Size? Food? Teeth?**

   Small/quick runner; plant-eater; soft/small teeth.

   b) The dinosaur called Stegosaurus had soft teeth, it couldn't run quickly, it couldn't swim, and it couldn't hide easily. How do you think it protected itself?

   Armour plating over body; spikes/horns on tail.

   c) The dinosaur called Anatosaurus had sharp teeth and webbed feet. What do you think it ate?

   Fish or something containing flesh that lived in swamps/water.

7. **a) List 2 types of animals that Tyrannosaurus could not catch and eat.**

   Birds, fish – couldn't fly or swim.

   b) The answer is dinosaur. List 4 questions with this answer.

   1. What is an extinct animal?
   2. What is the name for the gigantic animals that lived millions of years ago?
   3. What is the name of the huge animal whose fossils are found today?
   4. What is a Brontosaurus?

8. If scientists today created dinosaurs in the laboratory then ...

... they would be kept in zoos for people to see.

9. a) Why did the Diplodocus need such a long neck?

To reach leaves on trees.

b) Why did dinosaurs, like other reptiles, lay eggs rather than have live babies?

To keep its brain away from meat-eating dinosaurs.

10. Which two of the following statements are facts?

Statements b) and c).

11. Why is this poor reasoning? What is Sue assuming?

Sue assumes that one property (large size) automatically leads to another property (fierceness/aggressiveness).

12. Write down the three most important things for you to know before believing his story.

a)   Does he have a good professional reputation?
b)   Was anyone else with him?
c)   Were there any other dinosaur eggs found in the area?

14. Write in 1 to 5 words along each arrow in the diagram to make sensible sentences.

Starting from the top left (clockwise): had a small; were large; had bones found today as; gradually became; laid; could have been killed by.

www.ingramcontent.com/pod-product-compliance
Lightning Source LLC
Chambersburg PA
CBHW060227030426
42335CB00014B/1358